THE TOP 100
HEALTH
TIPS

THE TOP 100 HEALTH TIPS

JANET WRIGHT

DUNCAN BAIRD PUBLISHERS

LONDON

To my mother Marie Joan Wright and to my husband David Hall

THE TOP 100 HEALTH TIPS
Janet Wright

Distributed in the UK and USA in 2007 by
Duncan Baird Publishers Ltd
Sixth Floor, Castle House
75–76 Wells Street
London W1T 3QH

Conceived, created and designed by Duncan Baird Publishers

Managing Editor: Grace Cheetham
Editor: Dawn Bates
Managing Designer: Dan Sturges
Designer: Gail Jones
Commissioned photography: Toby Scott at Simon Smith studios

Library of Congress Cataloging-in-Publication Data available

ISBN: 978-1-84483-648-2

10 9 8 7 6 5 4 3 2 1

Typeset in Helvetica Condensed
Color reproduction by Colourscan, Singapore
Printed in Thailand by Imago

Publisher's Note: The information in this book is not intended as a substitute for professional medical advice and treatment. If
you are pregnant or breastfeeding or have any special dietary requirements, allergies or medical conditions, it is recommended
that you consult a medical professional before following any of the information or recipes contained in this book. Duncan Baird
Publishers, or any other persons who have been involved in working on this publication, cannot accept responsibility for any
errors or omissions, inadvertent or not, that may be found in the recipes or text, nor for any problems that may arise as a result
of preparing one of these recipes or following that advice contained in this work.

Notes on the recipes
Unless otherwise stated:
• Use large eggs • Use fresh herbs • 1 tsp = 5ml, 1 tbsp = 15ml, 1 cup = 225ml
• All recipes serve four.

CONTENTS

KEY TO SYMBOLS

- antioxidant
- antibacterial
- antiviral
- anti-inflammatory
- regulates hormones
- protects the heart
- anticancer
- antiaging
- good for the skin

Introduction

It really is possible to eat your way to good health and improve the way you feel and look. In *The Top 100 Health Tips* I've selected 100 delicious and nutritious foods you can easily introduce into your diet for maximum impact on your health.

In Chapter 1, Health Improvers, discover what to eat to boost your immune system, soothe inflammation, and speed up the healing process. The foods in Chapter 2, Detoxifiers and Digestion Soothers, help your digestion work more effectively, support the body's cleansing systems, combat ulcers, and cure nausea. They can also solve disorders such as indigestion, constipation, and irritable bowel syndrome. Chapter 3, Fitness Enhancers, includes eating strategies to provide sustained energy, improve performance, build and maintain strength, increase endurance, and turn your food to muscle rather than fat. It also helps to reduce the risk of sports injuries and mineral imbalances. Chapter 4, Weight Shifters, is packed with tasty foods that fill you up sooner and for longer, combat hormonal weight gain, and control blood-sugar. Some also help to burn off fat. Chapter 5, Brain Boosters and Mood Lifters, reveals how what you eat can improve your memory, libido, mood, sleeping patterns, and mental alertness. It includes food to combat symptoms of PMS and menopause. Chapter 6, Life Lengtheners, includes foods that combat chronic illness or conditions that strike in later life, such as cancers, heart disease, diabetes, arthritis, osteoporosis, and prostate disease. They also help keep your eyes and skin young.

A VARIED DIET

Particular foods can be very effective against certain health conditions, but they shouldn't be eaten to the exclusion of other fresh produce. Most fruit and vegetables, especially, will do you good, and their benefits are too wide-ranging to be strictly categorized. The risk of heart disease and cancer is reduced by a particularly wide range of foods: see the symbols on each page.

Many health conditions stem from nutrient deficiencies, so they can be alleviated—and often cured—by eating better. Base your diet on a wide range of vegetables and fruits, backed by wholegrain cereals and organic meat and dairy products, with as little processed food as possible.

STORING FOOD
Fresh fruit and vegetables lose much of their vitamin content in storage. So shop where you know food is fresh, keep it in a refrigerator or a cool place and eat as soon as possible. Keep fresh herbs in a clean screwtop jar with a pinch of salt, covered with olive oil, or for a few days in the fridge, wrapped in damp paper. Fresh meat should be placed on a plate on the bottom shelf of the refrigerator.

SUPPLEMENTS
It's always better to get your nutrients from a balanced diet, than by taking supplements. No one knows exactly how it works —only that the whole fruit or vegetable seems to provide a full range of nutrients in the right balance. Beta carotene, for example, is so good for the lungs that smokers who get plenty of it in their diet reduce their risk of lung cancer. Yet, taking beta carotene supplements seems

STAR FOODS
Kale for your immune system (see page 16)
Mussels to combat inflammation (see page 26)
Apples for digestive health (see page 32)
Green beans for fitness (see page 52)
Garlic for weight loss (see page 70)
Tofu for fat burning (see page 76)
Sea vegetables to improve emotional health (see page 86)
Flax seed to solve hormonal upheavals (see page 96)
Cherries for antiaging (see page 102)
Walnuts for your heart (see page 116)

to increase their cancer risk. It's almost impossible to overdose on the nutrients from fruit and vegetables, but it's easy to unbalance your levels of vitamins, and especially of minerals, if you take some of them in the large quantities supplied by supplements. The only exception is vitamin B12. Vegans who don't get enough of this from their diet should take this as part of a vitamin B-complex supplement.

EAT ORGANIC
Organic foods are produced in much the same way food was grown for thousands of years, until the twentieth century. Organic farmers don't use synthetic chemicals or sewage sludge. Their animals are given medicines only when they're unwell—not to make them put on weight faster or as a way of counteracting the unhealthy conditions of factory farms. Organic food has not been irradiated or genetically modified.

It's worth paying a little extra to eat organic, although the price difference is narrowing all the time. You'll avoid eating drug or chemical residues, and have a much lower risk of catching a disease such as food poisoning from chicken. Not all scientific studies have found that organic foods are more nutritious, but many have—and none has found them less healthy! Animal welfare standards are higher, too, and organic farming is very much kinder to the environment. If you can't afford to buy all organic goods, prioritize meat products and out of season fruits and vegetables.

INGREDIENTS

Buy as much produce as possible that is in season. Fruit and vegetables are at their most nutritious during the season when they naturally grow, and when they are bought from local sources so they are fresh when they reach you.

Stir-frying in a few tablespoons oil adds very little to the fat content, and helps the body to absorb fat-soluble vitamins, such as A and D. Leafy vegetables can be steamed in a couple of minutes, often less.

FLEXIBLE RECIPES

Many recipes in this book are based on traditional dishes from around the world.

Feel free to adjust the quantities and substitute the ingredients to suit your individual taste. That's part of the pleasure of cooking. Salt is rarely mentioned: season to taste, but if you do usually add salt, just give the recipes a try without.

SAFETY WARNING

- Wash all fruit and vegetables. Nonorganic should be well scrubbed or peeled; organic should be rinsed.
- Bean sprouts must be extra carefully washed, as their growing conditions may encourage growth of microbes.
- Beans, especially kidney beans, can be poisonous if not properly cooked. Canned beans are safe, easy, and just as nutritious as the fresh version. If using dry beans, soak them at least 5 hours, throw away the water and boil 10 minutes, then cook them for at least an hour in two to three times their volume of water. (Lentils don't need to be soaked beforehand.) Slow cookers don't get hot enough, and undercooked beans are even more poisonous than raw.
- Always clean seafood thoroughly, discarding any with shells that are broken or already open. When they are cooked, don't eat any that are still closed.
- Meat should be cooked through. Don't use too fierce a heat, though, as this can create chemical reactions linked with cancer.
- Don't dry-fry anything in a nonstick pan.
- If you may have any health condition, do check with your doctor before changing your diet.

⊙ ⑫ ⊙ ⊙ ⑪ ♡ ⊙ ◉ ●

cranberry

NUTRIENTS
Vitamins C, K; manganese; fiber

Bacteria come unstuck when faced with these tiny, but tasty, infection-fighting fruits.

One of the natural-health success stories of the past few years, cranberries have proved their value in preventing urinary tract infections, such as cystitis. Many people now eat them every day, as a first line of defense against these painful and dangerous conditions. The powerful ingredient is a flavonoid called proanthocyanidins, which is more abundant in cranberries than in most other fruit. Proanthocyanidins prevent bacteria sticking to the urinary tract wall, and prevent infections of the mouth and stomach in the same way.

> Soak dried fruit, such as currants and raisins, in cranberry juice for a tasty compote.

CRANBERRY SAUCE

²/₃ cup dried cranberries
1 cup cranberry
   or orange juice
1-in. piece gingerroot, finely
   chopped
1 tbsp. red wine (optional)
2 tbsp. honey

Place the cranberries and juice in a pan and soak 30 minutes. Bring to a boil, add the ginger and wine, if using, and simmer 10 minutes, stirring. Mix in the honey and serve with meat or a nut roast.

kiwi fruit

The vitamin-filled strength of these refreshing fruit will keep you breathing freely.

Bite for bite, there is more vitamin C in a ripe kiwi fruit than in most citrus fruits. And although vitamin C is well known for warding off colds, its effects go much farther than that. It protects the body from all kinds of infections and inflammation, and is particularly effective against respiratory diseases. Scientists have found it helps reduce coughing, wheezing, and rhinitis. People who eat kiwi fruit are less likely than others to suffer from asthma attacks, but it shouldn't be given to very small children as it can cause allergies. It is also good for the heart and vision. Eating kiwi fruits regularly has also been found to lower blood cholesterol and reduce the risk of blood clots.

NUTRIENTS
Vitamins C, E, beta carotene; copper, magnesium, potassium; fiber

KIWI AND AVOCADO SALAD

2 avocados, pitted and sliced
1 apple, cored and sliced
3 kiwi fruits, sliced
2 tsp. lemon juice
3 tbsp. olive oil
1 tbsp. wine vinegar
2 cups shredded lettuce

Place the avocados, apple, 2 of the kiwi fruits, and the lemon juice in a bowl and mix together. Crush the remaining kiwi fruit, blend with the olive oil and vinegar, and pour over the fruit. Serve on a bed of lettuce.

orange

NUTRIENTS
Vitamins A, B1, C, folate; calcium, potassium; fiber

This popular fruit is best known for its vitamin C content, but it also contains many other disease-fighting compounds.

Oranges are known for their immune-boosting power. A medium-size orange provides more than the average daily requirement of vitamin C, which fights off infections and strengthens the body's defenses. Particularly effective against colds and other respiratory ailments, including asthma, oranges have also been found to reduce the risk of stomach ulcers, kidney stones, and certain cancers. Their natural sugars help diabetics maintain their blood glucose levels. And a teaspoonful of grated organic orange peel added to food can reduce cholesterol. Citrus fruits also contain limonin, which is being researched for its anticancer and cholesterol-lowering possibilities.

ORANGE-YOGURT SUNDAE

4 tbsp. plain yogurt
grated peel of ½ orange
2 oranges, sliced into wheels
1 banana, sliced
1 tbsp. berries
¼ tsp. cinnamon

Mix together the yogurt and the peel and chill for an hour. In a separate bowl, mix together the fruit and cinnamon, then chill. Divide the fruit salad into bowls and spoon the yogurt over. Serve immediately.

⊙ ⦿ ⦿ ♥ ⊙ ◉ ⊜

raspberry

This tasty summer fruit might be small and delicate, but it has the power to protect against yeast infections and irritable bowel syndrome.

NUTRIENTS
Vitamins B2, B3, C, folate; copper, magnesium, manganese, potassium; fiber

The flavonoids called anthocyanins that give a raspberry its exquisite color are also responsible for some of its most valuable qualities. They have antimicrobial effects that can prevent the proliferation of bacteria and fungi in the digestive system. One of these, *Candida albicans*, causes the irritating vaginal infection called thrush and has also been linked with digestive disorders, such as irritable bowel syndrome. Like all berries, raspberries are also packed with antioxidants that promote overall health in the long term. They protect eyesight, reduce the risk of certain cancers, and their soluble fiber content helps to keep blood-sugar levels steady.

RASPBERRY SORBET

4 cups raspberries
juice and peel of 2 limes
2 tbsp. honey

Place the raspberries in a blender and puree. Strain through a cloth into a bowl and discard the pulp. Add the remaining ingredients and 1 cup water to the raspberries. Mix together and freeze 2 to 3 hours. Beat with a rolling pin or blend until it is a soft consistency, but not runny. Freeze again until set.

Brussels sprout

A small but powerful defender of the immune system, this crunchy vegetable easily punches above its weight in nutrients.

Brussels sprouts have huge health benefits. They are especially effective in supporting the immune system during the winter months when infections are most likely to strike. On top of their vitamin and mineral content, they contain numerous disease-fighting phytochemicals, including glucosinolates and antioxidant phenols. Glucosinolates are now believed to combat the carcinogens caused by overheating meat. Brussels sprouts are good for the skin, too, giving it a healthy, lustrous glow.

NUTRIENTS

Vitamins B1, B2, B6, C, E, K, beta carotene, folate; calcium, copper, iron, magnesium, manganese, phosphorus, potassium; fiber; omega-3 oils; protein

BRUSSELS SPROUTS WITH CHESTNUTS

4 slices bacon (optional)
14oz. Brussels sprouts, trimmed
14oz. chestnuts, cooked or vacuum-packed
2 tbsp. butter
salt and pepper to taste

Broil the bacon, if using, and cut into strips. Steam or boil the sprouts 5 minutes until cooked, but still crunchy. Drain the sprouts, add the chestnuts, butter, and the bacon strips, if using. Season and serve immediately.

carrot

This colorful vegetable might not actually make you see in the pitch dark, but it really is good for your eyes and overall vision.

The carrot is one of the richest sources of phytonutrients called carotenoids, which are responsible for its color and for a host of health benefits. These nutrients are what make carrots so good for the eyes, particularly for seeing in poor light. Carrots have tough cell walls that do not give up their nutrients easily. To get the best nutritional value, they should be juiced or cooked rather than eaten raw. Cooking them with oil allows the body to use more beta carotene.

Eating just one carrot a day might halve a smoker's risk of lung cancer.

NUTRIENTS
Vitamins C, K, beta carotene; potassium; fiber

CARROTS IN ORANGE

**1lb. carrots, cut
  into batons
1 tbsp. olive oil
1½ cups chopped onions
1 tsp. caraway seeds
4 tbsp. orange juice**

Parboil the carrots 5 minutes, then drain. Heat the oil in a pan and sauté the onion 3 minutes, then add the caraway seeds 2 minutes. Add the carrots, pour the juice over and turn up the heat until the juice boils. Reduce the heat and simmer 5 minutes, until most of the fluid evaporates. Serve immediately.

kale

NUTRIENTS
Vitamins B6, C, E, K, beta carotene; calcium, copper, manganese, potassium; fiber

COLORFUL KALE

1lb. carrots, cut into batons
1½ cups frozen corn kernels
5 cups roughly chopped kale leaves
1 bell pepper, seeded and cut into strips
salt and pepper to taste

Place 2 cups water in a saucepan. Add the carrots and bring to a boil, then simmer about 5 minutes. Add the frozen corn, kale, and pepper, and simmer 3 minutes longer. Season and serve immediately.

This leafy winter wonderfood will help to keep you healthy through the coldest time of the year.

Dark green leafy vegetables are highly nutritious, and kale is one of the top scorers. In winter your immune system comes under attack and this vitamin-C packed vegetable, providing your daily requirement in one large portion, is a potent defender against colds and viruses. Its anti-inflammatory effects also reduce the risk of asthma attacks and joint pains.

Kale in season has fewer pesticide residues, even if it is nonorganic.

Weatherproof health

As well as boosting immunity, kale provides bone-building calcium to counteract the weakening effects of being less active in winter, and lutein and zeaxanthin, which will protect your eyes in wintry conditions. It contains plenty of fiber to keep blood-sugar levels steady, in case staying indoors during the cold weather tempts you to eat more. And all this comes for less than 45 calories a portion. Meanwhile, its long-term benefits as an antioxidant, cleansing and reducing the risk of cancer, are stacked up in your favor, too.

Lifesaver

Kale is exceptionally rich in beta carotene. If you're a smoker, or a passive smoker, it might just save your life. A compound in cigarette smoke has been found to cause vitamin A deficiency, which can lead to lung diseases, including emphysema and cancer. But foods rich in beta carotene – which the body turns into vitamin A – can counteract these effects.

SESAME KALE

1 tbsp. sesame oil
2 cloves garlic, crushed
5 cups roughly chopped kale leaves
1 tsp. soy sauce
1 tbsp. toasted sesame seeds

Heat the oil in a pan and sauté the garlic 30 seconds over medium heat. Add the kale leaves and 2 tablespoons water and increase the heat, stirring frequently, until the water evaporates. Stir in the soy sauce and the sesame seeds just before serving.

800

onion

As strong in healing power as they are in taste, these vegetables keep disease at a safe distance.

The powerful anti-inflammatory effects of onions make them a vital ingredient in nourishing winter dishes. They are full of nutrients that counteract respiratory problems at all levels, from the nasal congestion caused by a cold to the wheezing of asthma. Their antibacterial action combats all kinds of infectious disease and they protect the digestive system, reducing the risk of intestinal growths that can lead to cancer. The same compounds cause the smell and the healing effects, so the more pungent the onion, the more good it will do you.

NUTRIENTS
Vitamins B6, C, folate; chromium, copper, manganese, molybdenum, phosphorus, potassium; fiber

ONION SOUP WITH CHEESY TOAST

4 tbsp. olive oil
6 large onions, thinly sliced
2 tbsp. all-purpose flour
2 qt. stock
2 tbsp. white wine
4 tbsp. grated cheese
4 slices French bread

Heat the oil in a pan and fry the onions until golden. Stir in the flour. Add the stock gradually and bring to a boil, stirring constantly. Add the wine and simmer 20 minutes. Sprinkle the cheese on the bread and toast under a broiler. Pour the soup into bowls and place the toast on top. Serve immediately.

600

◉ ✋ ♡ ⒸＧ ◉ ━

bell pepper

This versatile vegetable provides an amazing array of nutrients to help you see clearly and breathe freely.

NUTRIENTS
Vitamins B6, C, K, beta carotene, and other carotenoids

Peppers provide a healthy serving of immunity-boosting nutrients, including two antioxidants that work well together: beta carotene (the precursor of vitamin A) and vitamin C. Together, these offer protection against cell-damaging free radicals and protect the lungs from winter infections, asthma and even the ravages of second-hand smoke. Red peppers are especially high in cancer-fighting lycopene and in vitamin C and carotenoids, which protect vision and reduce the risk of eye diseases.

BROILED PEPPER AND WALNUT SALAD

4 bell peppers, seeded and cut into strips
handful walnut halves
2 tbsp. olive oil
1 tsp. vinegar
1 lettuce, roughly torn salt to taste

Heat the peppers under a hot broiler until the skin is black and blistered. When cool enough to touch, peel off the skin and discard. Heat the walnuts gently in 1 teaspoon oil in a skillet until crisp. Mix together the remaining oil, vinegar, and salt. Place the lettuce in a serving bowl and the peppers and walnuts on top. Pour the dressing over and serve while still warm.

⊙ ⬙ ✸ ♡

basil

NUTRIENTS
Vitamins A, C; calcium, iron, magnesium, manganese, potassium; fiber

Add the fresh leaves at the end of cooking to keep their flavor and their healthy effects.

TRICOLORE SALAD

1lb. cherry or napolina tomatoes, halved
1¾ cups cubed mozzarella
2 tbsp. balsamic vinegar
generous handful basil leaves

Mix together the tomatoes and mozzarella in a serving bowl, pour the vinegar over, and toss. Sprinkle the basil leaves on top and serve immediately.

This fragrant herb has antimicrobial effects that can reduce the risk of food poisoning.

Basil has long been used for healing: the Ayurvedic remedy tulsi is Holy basil (*Ocimum sanctum*), a close relative of our everyday Sweet basil (*Ocimum basilicum*). Basil leaves are rich in oils that reduce inflammation and kill harmful bacteria. Recent tests have found that these oils can counteract the growth of antibiotic-resistant superbugs, including those that cause food poisoning and others that infect wounds. As it was traditionally used as an anti-inflammatory remedy, its effects in that area are currently being studied. Around the house, a pot of basil is a traditional insect repellent.

◉ ⚕ ❁

clove

This fresh-tasting spice relieves toothache and sore mouths, and is a traditional remedy for bad breath.

Naturally antibacterial and anti-inflammatory, cloves are as likely to be found in herbal medicine chests as in the kitchen. They have long been used to numb the pain of toothache and, as well as having anesthetic effects, they combat the bacterial infection and inflammation that can lead to gum disease and the risk of additional damage to teeth. The oil in cloves contains a compound called eugenol that has long been used by dentists, and oil of cloves is still kept for that purpose in many homes. The anti-inflammatory properties of eugenol may protect other parts of the body, too, including joints.

NUTRIENTS
Vitamin C; calcium, magnesium, manganese; fiber; omega-3 oils

BAKED APPLES

heaped 4 tbsp. raisins or
   golden raisins
1 tsp. ground nutmeg
4 large unpeeled cooking
   apples, cored, skin scored
   around middle
4 tsp. cloves
1 tbsp. butter (optional)

Heat the oven to 375°F. Mix the fruit with the nutmeg and stuff the mixture into each apple. Stud the skins with cloves and place in a greased baking tray. Pour 1 tablespoon water over each apple and place a little butter on top, if using. Bake 25 minutes, or until soft, basting occasionally. Serve the apples on their own or with cream.

◉ ◔ ✪ ♡

coriander/cilantro

This versatile ingredient reduces the dangerous effects of hot weather on food.

NUTRIENTS

Iron, magnesium, manganese; fibre

Coriander is unusual in that its leaves, also called cilantro, are used as a herb and its groundup seeds as a spice. Both have long been popular among cooks in hot countries, especially where it is difficult to protect meat from heat and flies. Scientists have discovered the reason behind the traditional lore: coriander offers protection against food poisoning. It contains antibacterial compounds that protect against numerous bugs, including some of the most dangerous, such as salmonella. Ayurvedic healers use coriander for its anti-inflammatory effects.

EGYPTIAN GREENS SOUP

1 qt. stock
8 cups roughly torn spinach
1 tbsp. olive oil
4 tsp. coriander seeds, ground
4 cloves garlic, crushed
½ tsp. salt
1 tsp. vinegar (optional)
2 tbsp. finely chopped cilantro
    leaves

Bring the stock to a boil in a large pan. Add the spinach, bring back to a boil and simmer 5 minutes. Heat the oil in a skillet and fry the coriander seeds, garlic, and salt 1 to 2 minutes until the garlic starts to brown. Add to the spinach with the vinegar, if using. Stir and sprinkle with cilantro. Serve immediately.

013

◎ ✋ ♡ ©

mustard

Valued for its warming effects, this plant has many ways of protecting the lungs.

Mustard seeds have long been used to relieve respiratory ailments. They are rich in selenium and magnesium, two key nutrients often lacking in modern diets, which both help to reduce inflammation in the lungs and ease the symptoms of asthma. A mustard-seed poultice on the chest can also help to rid the lungs of mucus. Less commonly used than the seeds, mustard leaves are rich in other nutrients, including vitamin C and beta carotene, that improve lung function and help protect against the harmful effects of secondhand tobacco smoke.

NUTRIENTS
Vitamin B3; calcium, iron, magnesium, manganese, phosphorous, selenium, zinc; fiber; omega-3 oils; protein

VINAIGRETTE DRESSING

2 tsp. mustard seeds
1 tsp. salt
2 cloves garlic (optional)
2 tbsp. balsamic or wine
 vinegar
6 tbsp. olive oil

Crush the mustard seeds with a mortar and pestle, or in a spice grinder, then add the salt and garlic, if using, and crush again. Transfer to a bowl, pour in the vinegar and olive oil, and beat together.

turmeric

Prized for its color, this spice is actually one of the most health-protective ingredients in a curry.

NUTRIENTS
Vitamin B6; iron, manganese, potassium

Served with cruciferous vegetables, turmeric increases protection against prostate cancer.

Many spices would have excellent effects if they were not eaten in such small quantities. Turmeric, however, is such a strong anti-inflammatory that the small amount used in a curry is enough to reduce the risk of illness. The potent ingredient is curcumin, which gives turmeric its vivid golden color. It has been shown to protect against inflammatory bowel disease and several forms of cancer, relieve the pain and stiffness of arthritis, and improve liver function. Turmeric can also counteract the carcinogenic effects of some additives that are found in processed food.

SPICED CAULIFLOWER

1 large cauliflower, broken
  into flowerets
1 tbsp. peanut oil
1 tsp. ground coriander
1 tsp. ground black pepper
1 large onion, chopped
1 tsp. salt
1 tbsp. turmeric

Steam the cauliflower 10 minutes. Meanwhile, heat the oil in a pan over low heat and briefly fry the coriander and black pepper. Add the onion and stir-fry 3 to 5 minutes until translucent. Add the salt and turmeric. Stir in the cauliflower until well coated and serve.

chickpea

Rich in minerals that support the metabolic process, chickpeas keep you up to speed with a busy life.

The need for essential minerals, especially iron, increases when you're overworking, not least to help your body ward off infection. Women, in particular, tend to be deficient in iron until menopause ends their monthly blood loss. If, like many people, you've cut down on red meat, you could be short of this vital mineral. Chickpeas, or garbanzos, provide plenty of iron, as well as helping to stabilize blood sugar. They also help the body deal with preservatives, found in some fast foods, that can cause headaches. Canned chickpeas (without added sugar or salt) are just as nutritious as dried.

NUTRIENTS
Folate; copper, iron, manganese, molybdenum, phosphorus; fiber; protein

HUMMUS

1 can (15-oz.) chickpeas, drained
2 cloves garlic, crushed
3 tbsp. lemon juice
2 tbsp. tahini (sesame seed paste)
2 tbsp. olive oil

Blend the chickpeas with the garlic and lemon juice, or mash them in a bowl. Stir in the tahini and oil and add a little water for smoothness, if wished. Serve with wholewheat bread or crudités.

⊙ ✋ ◐ ◑ ♥ C ◉ ◉ ≋

mussel

NUTRIENTS
Vitamins B2, B6, B12, E, folate; iron, potassium, selenium, zinc

The dynamic duo of selenium and omega-3 fatty acids makes the often-overlooked mussel a nutritional superstar.

A weekly meal of mussels can help bring everyday ailments, such as asthma, eczema, and joint pain, under control, and help to prevent hormonal upheaval. Mussels are rich in minerals, including selenium (hard to find in most diets), that reduce inflammation. Another powerful anti-inflammatory effect comes from omega-3 fatty acids, and mussels are richer in omega-3 than other shellfish. Both selenium and omega-3 help to regulate hormone production too. Omega-3's numerous good results include protecting

MUSSEL SOUP

2lb. 4oz. mussels, cleaned
1½ qt. fish stock or water
1 tbsp. olive oil
1 large onion, chopped
1 large carrot, diced
1 stick celery, chopped
½ cup white wine
salt and pepper to taste

Boil the mussels in the stock in a covered pan until the shells open; remove and discard the shells and any that haven't opened. Heat the oil and sauté the vegetables 5 minutes. Strain the stock, then add to the vegetables. Add the wine, bring to a boil, and simmer 10 minutes until the vegetables are soft. Add the mussels, season, and serve immediately.

MUSSELS WITH SALSA

4 tomatoes, diced
4 cloves garlic, crushed
2 small chilies, seeded and chopped
2 green bell peppers, seeded and chopped
juice of 2 lemons
2 tbsp. olive oil

16 mussels, cleaned

To make the salsa, mix all the ingredients, except the mussels, and chill. Steam the mussels until the shells are all open; discard any unopened and serve with the salsa and fresh bread.

against cancer and heart disease, preventing cell damage, and improving brain function.

The right choice

We're advised to eat oily fish 2 to 3 times a week, but some species are overfished, while others swim in polluted waters. Mussels, being sustainably farmed, offer a safe alternative. Follow the safety advice on page 9 when eating seafood.

Mussels contain twice as much iron, weight for weight, as red meat.

venison

NUTRIENTS
Vitamins B2, B3, B6, B12; copper, iron, phosphorus, selenium, zinc; protein

For the strengthening and energy-boosting benefits of red meat with little fat, eat venison.

Meat from deer and their relatives is packed with protein, minerals, and B vitamins. Because of the low fat content, it is much healthier than other red meat and is the ideal ingredient to boost depleted iron stores. Venison's abundant B vitamins help the body store energy and can protect against migraines. These vitamins play numerous other roles, too, such as protecting against bone disorders and certain cancers.

> Venison is one of the richest sources of vitamin B12, which is hard to find except in meat.

MARINATED VENISON

2 tbsp. olive oil
4 tbsp. dry red wine
1 tbsp. chopped rosemary
1 tbsp. chopped thyme
4 cloves garlic, crushed
4 venison steaks

Mix together the oil, red wine, herbs and garlic in a nonmetallic bowl. Pour over the steaks in a nonmetallic dish and marinate for at least an hour, turning occasionally. Broil the steaks under medium heat until cooked through. Serve.

honey

This versatile food will help to heal a wound, promote digestion, and prevent mouth ulcers.

Honey has been used as a healing agent throughout history. Daubing an ulcer or wound with honey speeds recovery because of its antiseptic qualities and because it has a drying effect that inhibits the growth of fungi and bacteria. It can also reduce the risk of gum disease. Eating it is also valuable as it can improve digestion, and recent research suggests it can counteract food-poisoning bacteria. The bees' food sources affect the honey—its healing powers are increased if they feed on particularly healthy plants, such as the New Zealand manuka bush.

NUTRIENTS
Vitamins B2, B6; iron, manganese

HONEY VINAIGRETTE

2 tbsp. honey
2 tbsp. apple cider vinegar
3 tbsp. extra virgin olive oil
1 tsp. French mustard
   (optional)
pinch salt

Pour the honey and vinegar into a pan and place over low heat until just warm. Add the olive oil, beating the mixture with a fork. Remove from the heat, then add the mustard and salt. Serve with a warm salad, such as chicken.

◉ ◍ ◍ ♥ Ⓒ ◉ ≣

lemon

NUTRIENTS
Vitamin C; flavonoids; limonin

Nothing tastes fresher than lemon, which has amazing cleansing and antioxidant powers.

Despite its sourness, lemon juice is a popular drink when diluted in water, with a cleansing taste few other fruits can match. During a brief detox fast, it quells the appetite and freshens breath. Used in a marinade or dressing, lemon aids digestion by breaking down some of the tough components of meat. Its calming effects on the digestive system relieve bloating and heartburn. It also has a slightly antibacterial effect, reducing the risk of discomfort in the intestines. Packed with vitamin C, lemon's powerful antioxidant effects strengthen all the body's cells, aiding detoxification.

TANGY FISH

**4 skinless tuna or other
fish fillets
peel and juice of 1 lemon
peel and juice of 1 lime
2 tbsp. olive oil
2 tsp. finely snipped chives
1 tsp. ground black pepper**

Heat the broiler and place the fish on a foil-lined broiler pan. Mix the peels with the oil and coat each fillet. Broil 8 to 10 minutes, until cooked through, turning once. Mix together the juices, chives, and pepper. Pour the mixture over the fish and serve immediately.

prune

Dried plums regulate the digestive system, speeding it up or slowing it down—whichever is needed.

Containing many of the same nutrients as fresh plums, prunes also have a beneficial effect on the digestive system. They have long been used as the most effective, yet gentle, natural remedy for constipation. Their fiber-rich bulk softens food waste that has dried out during an excessive delay in the colon, and helps it move painlessly on and out of the body. Yet, prunes can also slow the movement of food from the stomach if it is emptying too quickly, causing indigestion or wind. Prunes lower cholesterol by helping the body to excrete fats, and feed the good bacteria in the intestine, helping to prevent harmful bacteria breeding.

NUTRIENTS
Beta carotene; copper, potassium; fiber

DRIED FRUIT COMPOTE

heaped 2 tbsp. chopped prunes
2 tbsp. chopped dried apple
2 tbsp. dried berries or other
dried fruit
1 tsp. lemon juice

Put all the ingredients in a bowl and cover with water; refrigerate overnight. Stir well and serve for breakfast, topped with yogurt.

apple

NUTRIENTS
Vitamins C, K; fiber; flavonoids

This fruit works wonders for both detox and digestion thanks to the combination of pectin and fiber.

Apples have a huge number of health benefits, and scientists are only just starting to identify their numerous life-enhancing nutrients, but their superstar role is in digestion and detoxification. Eating an apple aids a detox by helping you feel full sooner and for longer, and can alleviate even chronic constipation, a widespread problem often caused by poor nutrition. Constipation prevents the body getting rid of toxins and can lead to more serious conditions, from hemorrhoids to colon cancer.

Gentle gel

Apples are rich in soluble and insoluble fiber, both of which help food progress at a healthy pace through the digestive system. These fibers pick up toxic waste, such as heavy metals, along the way—as well as cholesterol, which is one reason why apples are also good for the arteries. The toxins and cholesterol can then be safely excreted, with the help of the soluble fiber, pectin. It forms a gel-like substance that softens the body's waste and helps it leave the body naturally. Pectin has a regulating effect on the speed of digestion, slowing it down as

---

APPLE CHARLOTTE

2¼lb. cooking apples, cored and sliced
2 tbsp. honey
½ tsp. cinnamon
pinch nutmeg
8 slices bread, buttered both sides

Heat the oven to 375°F. Heat the apples with 2 tablespoons water in a pan, stirring until a thick puree. Stir in the honey, cinnamon, and nutmeg. Line the sides and bottom of a greased cake pan with half the bread, spoon the purée in, and top with the remaining bread. Bake for 30 minutes until golden brown. Serve immediately.

well as speeding it up when necessary. Its gel-like effects can also alleviate diarrhea, which removes food from the system too quickly for vital nutrients to be absorbed and can lead to dangerous levels of dehydration.

Apple peel is also rich in quercetin, which reduces the risk of sun damage to skin.

artichoke

This spiky little plant can hold a soothing answer to irritable bowel syndrome.

NUTRIENTS
Vitamins B6, C; calcium, iron, magnesium, manganese, phosphorus, potassium; fiber

The rich fiber content of artichoke aids digestion. If you suffer from indigestion or irritable bowel syndrome, artichoke might relieve symptoms, such as abdominal pain, flatulence, nausea, constipation, and diarrhea. It works by stimulating the flow of bile, a substance that helps to digest fat and encourages healthy movement of the intestine. This also prevents toxins building up in the liver and reduces the risk of gallstones. Eating an artichoke can reduce the effects of eating rich food.

FRESH ARTICHOKE

4 globe artichokes, outer leaves and stem removed
8 tbsp. vinaigrette (see p.23)

Boil the artichokes in salted water 30 to 40 minutes until you can pull off the leaves easily, drain and leave to cool. To eat, pull off the leaves and dip into the vinaigrette. Bite off the fleshy part with your teeth and discard the leaf. Cut out the hairy "choke" and eat the heart.

beet

The nutrient that gives beet its distinctive color has detoxifying and cancer-fighting powers.

The brilliant ruby hue of a beet has given it a traditional reputation as a blood cleanser. It certainly aids cell cleansing by increasing the liver's production of detoxifying enzymes, and the betacyanin that makes beets red is particularly effective in combating cancerous changes, too. Beet is a popular component of juice fasts, when mixed with a sweeter juice, such as apple, to dilute the taste. Scientists have found that the juice combats the effects of nitrates—chemical preservatives in processed meats that can cause colon cancer.

NUTRIENTS
Vitamin C, folate; copper, iron, magnesium, manganese, potassium, phosphorus; fiber

BEET SOUP

2 tbsp. olive oil
1 onion, chopped
2 cloves garlic, crushed
4 large beets, chopped
2 carrots, chopped
1 qt. stock
4 tbsp. plain yogurt

Heat the oil in a large pan and gently fry the onion 2 to 3 minutes, then add the garlic and cook for another minute. Add the beets, carrots, and stock and bring to a boil. Cover and simmer about 45 minutes, until soft. Puree, then ladel into bowls and top with yogurt.

broccoli

A potent defender against stomach ulcers, broccoli banishes harmful bacteria.

NUTRIENTS
Vitamins A, B6, C, E, K, folate; magnesium, phosphorus, potassium; fiber

As well as aiding the body's detoxification processes, broccoli is rich in a compound called sulforaphane, which strengthens the ability of cells to resist damage. It has recently been found to improve digestion by fighting the unusually tough bacterium *Helicobacter pylori*. Not only does this bacterium thrive in the stomach acid that kills most bacteria, but it can even, in some cases, withstand antibiotics. Eating away at the stomach lining, it creates ulcers that can develop into cancer. Broccoli counteracts the painful effects, and can even reduce the amount of harmful bacteria in the stomach.

BROCCOLI WITH ALMONDS

1lb. broccoli flowerets
1 tsp. olive oil
½ cup slivered almonds
juice of 1 lemon
2 tbsp. broccoli sprouts (optional)

Steam the broccoli flowerets for 5–10 minutes until they are just tender. Meanwhile, heat the olive oil in a pan over low heat and fry the almonds until brown. Mix together the broccoli and almonds in a serving dish and sprinkle the lemon juice over. Top the dish with broccoli sprouts, if using.

cauliflower

These delicate flowerets provide powerful backup for the liver in cleansing the body.

NUTRIENTS
Vitamins B5, B6, C, folate; manganese; fiber; omega-3 oils

One of the cruciferous family of vegetables, cauliflower has many health-giving attributes, including the ability to aid cell detoxification. Processed food is full of manufactured chemicals, and even healthy food can contain elements that have harmful side effects if they linger in the body. The liver works hard to filter out these toxins, which can cause cell damage leading to cancer and other diseases, and is helped by cauliflower, which is rich in antioxidants. But cauliflower's most powerful effects come from compounds, such as glucosinolates, that fuel and strengthen the liver during all stages of detoxification.

One large serving of cauliflower provides all the vitamin C you need in a day.

CAULIFLOWER PROVENÇALE

1 tbsp. olive oil
1 large onion, chopped
2 cloves garlic, crushed
2 small zucchini, diced
1 can (15-oz.) tomatoes
1 large cauliflower, cut
   into flowerets

Heat the oil and fry the onion 2 to 3 minutes. Stir in the garlic, add the zucchini and tomatoes and simmer 5 to 10 minutes. Meanwhile, steam the cauliflower 5 to 10 minutes until tender. Place in a serving dish. Pour the sauce over, and serve.

cucumber

NUTRIENTS
Vitamins A, C, folate; magnesium, manganese, molybdenum, potassium, silica; fiber

This crunchy salad vegetable, packed with mineral-rich fluid, aids digestion by keeping you hydrated.

The rich fiber content of cucumbers keeps the digestive system moving and, unlike some other high-fiber foods, comes balanced with its own supply of fluid. Eating cucumbers can ease or prevent constipation, which is often caused by not drinking enough. It's helpful, too, if you've had diarrhea, because as well as rehydrating it replaces vital minerals. Fresh cucumber juice can also alleviate acid indigestion. Cucumber's minerals are clustered in the peel, but the flesh, famed for soothing irritated skin, is rich in vitamin C and caffeic acid, which reduces inflammation.

CUCUMBER AND MINT SALAD

4 tbsp. chopped mint, plus a few leaves for garnish
1 large cucumber, chopped
2 stalks celery, chopped
2 tsp. white wine vinegar
8 tbsp. low-fat yogurt

Mix together the chopped mint, cucumber, and celery in a serving bowl. In a separate bowl, whisk the vinegar into the yogurt. Pour the dressing over the salad, garnish with mint leaves, and serve.

curly endive

This traditional remedy might taste bitter, but it has sweetly soothing effects on digestion.

These distinctive leaves contain intybin, which stimulates the appetite and prepares the digestive system to cope with rich food. It is this compound that gives curly endive its slightly bitter taste (the sharper the taste, the greater the benefits), and makes it an appetizing first course. Curly endive also has detoxifying effects, acting as a tonic to the liver and gallbladder. Its diuretic actions help the body eliminate toxins through increased urination. Its relatives (including other endives, chicories, and raddichio) have some of the same effects.

NUTRIENTS
Vitamins A, B-complex, beta carotene; iron, potassium

SUPER SALAD

4 curly endive leaves, shredded
4 red radicchio leaves, shredded
2 small Belgian (white) endives, separated
2 pears, cored and diced
8 shelled walnuts
honey vinaigrette (see p.29)

Toss all the ingredients together and dress with some honey vinaigrette. Serve immediately.

watercress

The peppery taste of these dark leaves gives a hint of their stimulating power.

Packed with nutrients, watercress has long been valued for its medicinal properties. It is a mild diuretic, preventing the discomfort of fluid retention by helping the kidneys pass more urine. As a traditional cleansing remedy, it is considered to support liver function and purify the blood—with improved skin quality as a visible result. Scientists have just started understanding its truly detoxifying effects: watercress contains some of the strongest anticancer nutrients found in plants. These compounds—including phenylethylisothiocyanate, or PEITC, which gives watercress its distinctive peppery taste—help in two stages of cell detoxification by rendering carcinogens harmless.

STIR-FRIED WATERCRESS WITH ALMONDS AND GINGER

4 tbsp. slivered almonds
2 tbsp. sesame oil
4 cups chopped watercress
2-in. piece finely chopped gingeroot
4 tbsp. miso
4 tbsp. rice vinegar

Heat a wok or skillet and dry-fry the almond; set aside. Add the oil to the wok and stir-fry the watercress and ginger 3 minutes. Add the miso, rice vinegar, and the almonds and stir well. Serve immediately.

black pepper

This underrated spice has a dual action in speeding toxins out of the body through sweat and urine.

Black pepper aids digestion and detoxification in several ways. Its spicy taste stimulates the taste buds, encouraging the body to secrete more hydrochloric acid, which breaks food down in the stomach. If the body doesn't produce enough hydrochloric acid, food can stay in the stomach for too long, causing feelings of indigestion. Or, it can be only partly digested when it moves on into the intestines, where it will produce wind and might lead to diarrhea. Black pepper's action promotes complete digestion. Peppery foods also increase the production of urine, in which toxins filtered by the kidneys are removed from the body. And pepper's warming effects increase perspiration, another route for elimination.

NUTRIENTS
Vitamin K; iron, manganese; fiber

Black pepper is believed to speed up fat burning by stimulating metabolic processes.

BLACK PEPPER RICE

1½ cups basmati rice
2 tbsp. black peppercorns
2 tsp. mustard seeds
2 tbsp. peanut oil
1 cup cashew nuts
½ tsp. turmeric

Boil the rice 10 minutes. Dry-fry the peppercorns and seeds 2 minutes; grind in a mortar and pestle. Heat the oil, add the nuts and turmeric and stir-fry 2 minutes. Stir in peppercorns, seeds, and rice. Serve.

cumin seed

This tasty spice has a distinctive warm fragrance and is an effective digestive aid.

NUTRIENTS
Iron, manganese

Cumin has long been valued in Asia and the Middle East for its digestive benefits. It relieves wind and can prevent digestive upsets, such as diarrhea. Medical science has now suggested a reason why: these small seeds—greenish-brown, black, and white—stimulate the production of pancreatic enzymes that help the body break down foods and absorb the nutrients. It kills many food-borne bacteria and supports the liver in its detoxifying processes. Chewing a few seeds sweetens the breath after eating meat. End a meal by chewing a blend of cumin, fennel, and cardamom seeds and cloves.

CUMIN CARROTS

1 tbsp. cumin seeds
3½ cups carrots, cut into batons
1 tbsp. peanut oil
2 cloves garlic, crushed
2 tbsp. white wine

Dry-fry the seeds briefly in a pan, and grind in a mortar and pestle or spice grinder. Boil the carrots 5 minutes until nearly tender; drain. Heat the oil in a skillet and sauté the garlic 1 minute. Add the wine and carrots and cook until the wine evaporates. Stir in the cumin and serve immediately.

ginger

The best and gentlest remedy for nausea, this is a mainstay for travelers and pregnant women.

Keeping ginger cookies to hand during early pregnancy is a piece of advice that's been handed down for generations. Ginger has now been recognized by scientists as a fast-acting cure for nausea of all kinds, more effective than routinely used drugs. It's also a traditional cure for indigestion. Ginger's warming effects promote detoxification by increasing sweat. It is also a powerful anti-inflammatory that can relieve the pain of arthritis and its active ingredients, gingerols, can kill cancer cells. For strongest effects, pour hot water on a thumb-size piece of peeled, crushed fresh gingerroot and drink it as a tea.

NUTRIENTS
Vitamin B6; copper, magnesium, manganese, potassium

SWEET-AND-SOUR VEGETABLES

1 large onion, chopped
2 tbsp. peanut oil
2 cloves garlic, crushed
2-in. piece gingerroot, finely chopped
4 tbsp. apple juice
6 cups chopped non-root vegetables of choice
2 tbsp. soy sauce

Heat the oil in a wok and fry the onion 2 to 3 minutes. Add the garlic, ginger, and apple juice and cook 3 minutes. Add the vegetables and stir-fry until tender. Stir in the soy sauce just before serving.

◎ ❧ ✿ ⓒ

peppermint

NUTRIENTS
Vitamins A, B2, C, folate; calcium, copper, iron, magnesium, manganese, potassium; fiber; omega-3 oils

> Garnish salads and cooked foods with fresh mint leaves to aid digestion.

This popular and fragrant herb has soothing effects on the muscles of the digestive system.

From a bunch of fresh leaves to a bag of candy, any form of peppermint can relieve digestive upsets fast. It soothes the burning pain of indigestion, kills bacteria, relieves wind, and regulates intestinal movement. Its ability to stop muscle spasm makes it a useful remedy for irritable bowel syndrome and for the abdominal cramps felt during painful periods. Use it with caution if you suffer from heartburn (when stomach acids rise into the throat), as although peppermint helps many sufferers, others find that it makes heartburn worse.

MINT TEA

4 tbsp. finely chopped peppermint
1-in. piece gingerroot, finely chopped
2 tsp. honey

Boil 2 cups water and pour over the mint and ginger; leave to steep until the liquid is cool enough to drink. Stir in the honey and drink when fully dissolved.

yogurt

This stomach-soothing food can provide dairy benefits to people who can't drink milk.

Some people are unable to digest dairy products because their body doesn't produce an enzyme called lactase. However, because the culture in yogurt produces its own lactase it can be enjoyed by most people. Yogurt also promotes the growth of beneficial bacteria in the intestines. Probiotic yogurts aim to help even more by having the starter culture still alive, and are sometimes supplemented with other cultures. Eating yogurt can combat the bacterium that causes stomach ulcers.

NUTRIENTS
Vitamins B2, B5, B12; calcium, iodine, molybdenum, phosphorus, potassium, zinc; protein

Eating yogurt can reduce the risk of catching stomach bugs while on vacation.

YOGURT WITH NUTS AND HONEY

1¾ cups yogurt
handful walnut halves
4 tbsp. honey
4 tbsp almonds

Mix the yogurt with the walnuts in a bowl. Drizzle the honey in a spiral over the top. Sprinkle with almonds and serve.

grape

A combination of grapes and bite-size cheese cubes make a great post-workout reviver.

This juicy and refreshing fruit is easy to snack on—it is energizing and replaces the essential minerals you lose during a workout.

HHWhen fitting in food before exercise is a problem, grapes provide a refreshing solution. Exercising soon after a meal is a recipe for indigestion, but if you work out on an empty stomach you'll have little energy to use. Grapes, an ideal pre-workout snack, are light, rich in quick-energy carbohydrate and easily digestible, and they replenish some of the fluid and minerals you'll lose as you sweat. It helps if you can keep them in your pocket and nibble them as you go along. Grapes also keep your heart strong by lowering harmful cholesterol.

REFRESHING GRAPE SALAD

1 tsp. olive oil
1 tbsp. wine vinegar
2 apples, cored and chopped
1 cup seedless grapes
1 small cucumber, chopped

Mix together the oil and vinegar in a bowl to make a dressing. Mix together the apples, grapes, and cucumber, pour the dressing over, and serve.

pineapple

A versatile enzyme in this refreshing fruit can help to heal the aches, pains, and bruises that often result from playing sports.

NUTRIENTS
Vitamins B1, B6, C; copper, manganese; fiber

Snacking on pineapple can help the body to heal faster, thanks to the plentiful nutrients it contains. One enzyme in particular, called bromelain, works as a powerful anti-inflammatory. It reduces the risk of inflammation when joints and muscles have been overworked or suffered minor damage. Backed by pineapple's rich vitamin C content, it also helps the body heal faster from bumps and bruises. The same action eases the pain of inflammatory conditions, such as arthritis and sore throats. Fresh pineapple is most effective, as processing reduces bromelain's strength.

PINEAPPLE SALSA

1 small pineapple
1 red onion, diced
1 tsp. lemon juice
2-in. piece gingerroot, finely
    chopped
1 tbsp. chopped mint

Remover the outer skin and chop the pineapple. Stir in the onion, lemon juice, ginger, and mint. Chill for up to 12 hours. Serve with cold meats or fish.

◎ ✋ ♥ ℂ ◉ ▬

watermelon

Much more than just the juiciest way to rehydrate after a workout, this refreshing fruit wards off any ill effects of exercise.

NUTRIENTS
Vitamins B1, B6, C, beta carotene; potassium, magnesium; lycopene

Watermelon contains minerals that help your body use its fluid most effectively, but it's doing far more than just replenishing fluid. It gives a healthy dose of energizing B vitamins to keep you going. Packed with anti-inflammatory vitamin C, it also helps to soothe overworked body tissues. And it is rich in lycopene, a powerful antioxidant that can prevent the cell damage caused by free radicals released during exercise. Unlike many fruits, watermelon loses little of its nutritional value when it's cut, so slices can be kept in the refrigerator for a few days.

WATERMELON REVIVER

**4 unwaxed oranges
½ cup plain yogurt
4 bananas, sliced
½ lb. watermelon, seeded
  and chopped**

Grate the orange peel and mix with the yogurt. Peel the oranges and slice into wheels. Layer the oranges and bananas in 4 glass bowls. Top with the watermelon and pour the yogurt mixture over. Serve.

⊙ ⊘ ⊙ ✋ ⊕ ♥ © ◉ ≋

alfalfa sprout

All types of sprouts are nutritious and energy-giving, but the tiny, delicate alfalfa variety is the best of a very good bunch.

Packed with nutrients, sprouts provide a burst of energy to see you through a workout. Alfalfa is one of the most nutritious, and it contains a compound that inhibits fungal growth, an occasional by-product of sweaty environments. Alfalfa sprouts are an unusually concentrated source of nutrients. The exact content of other sprouts varies according to the kind of bean they sprouted from, but all are nutritious. Rich in enzymes and fiber, they are easy to digest and contain very few calories.

NUTRIENTS
Vitamins B-complex, C, D, E, K; calcium, iron, potassium, zinc; fiber

SPROUT SALAD

8 large lettuce leaves
½ lb. alfalfa sprouts
4 stalks celery, chopped
1 large cucumber, diced
4 tbsp. vinaigrette (see p.23)
4 tbsp. seeds or nuts

Line 4 bowls with the lettuce leaves. Rinse the sprouts and add the celery and cucumber. Pour the vinaigrette dressing over, sprinkle the seeds or nuts over, and serve.

038

◉ ❀ ♥ ©

celery

NUTRIENTS
Vitamins B1, B2, B6, C, beta carotene, folic acid; calcium, iron, magnesium, manganese, molybdenum, phosphorus potassium; fiber

This crunchy fitness snack counteracts the dangers of drinking too much water during a workout.

A stalk of celery is the athlete's secret weapon because it's rich in a string of nutrients that keep energy levels high. It's an excellent source of vitamin C, which aids recovery from sports injuries by strengthening cell walls. Celery also has a slightly diuretic effect. And being higher in sodium than most vegetables (although nowhere near a harmful level), celery can prevent the dangerous mineral imbalance that results from drinking too much water during an energetic workout.

Stalks of celery stuffed with fromage blanc or low-fat soft cheese makes a great snack on the run.

CELERY AND BLUE CHEESE SALAD

1 tbsp. lemon juice
1 tbsp. olive oil
½ tsp. salt
2 apples, cored and chopped
2 stalks celery, chopped
1 bulb fennel, sliced
½ cup diced blue cheese, such as Stilton

Mix together the juice, oil, and salt. Pour over the apples, celery, and fennel and top with cheese. Serve immediately with crusty bread.

◎ ♥ ⒸC

potato

This staple vegetable is packed with vitamins and other energizing nutrients.

Don't overlook the value of potatoes if you're aiming to get fit. They're rich in vitamin B6, which—among many other essential services—is needed to mobilize the body's glycogen stores and help protein to build muscle. They are also packed with complex carbohydrates, the best form of energy food. Complex carbs play two roles, both essential to fitness. By providing slow-burning fuel, they give you enough energy to complete your workout without flagging halfway through. And they help the body to maintain the muscle it has built. Peeling removes many nutrients, so eat potatoes in their skins.

NUTRIENTS
Vitamins B6, C; copper, manganese potassium; fiber

TUNISIAN POTATOES WITH EGGS

4 eggs
3 cups diced potatoes
juice of 1 lemon
2 tbsp. cumin
2 tbsp. olive oil
½ tsp. harissa

Boil the eggs 10 minutes; leave to cool, then peel and chop. Boil the potatoes 5 to 10 minutes until tender; drain. Mix together the lemon juice, cumin, oil and harissa and pour over the potatoes. Place the potatoes on top of the eggs and serve immediately.

green bean

GREEN BEAN SALAD

2 eggs (optional)
1½ cups diced waxy potatoes
5oz. green beans, trimmed
juice of ½ lemon
1 tbsp. walnut oil
black pepper to taste

Boil the eggs, if using, 10 minutes. Boil the potatoes 5 to 10 minutes; drain. Blanch the beans in boiling water and remove while still crisp. Peel and chop the eggs, if using, and mix together with the potatoes and beans, when cool. Mix the lemon juice and oil, and pour over the salad. Season with pepper and serve.

These nutritional power-packs hold many benefits for anyone doing exercise.

Runner beans and their close relatives, string or thin green beans, are a rich source of the nutrients required for exercise. Although each of these nutrients is valuable individually, their powers are multiplied when many are contained in one food. The kind of range found in green beans allows them to work together in building and maintaining peak fitness. The vitamin K content, for example, promotes the healing of scrapes and cuts, while vitamin C backs this up by maintaining the strength of cell walls. The B vitamins work together to keep nerves functioning well and energy levels high.

Eat the freshest young green beans – straight from the plant is best.

Pumping iron

Green beans are packed with essential minerals: manganese and magnesium contribute toward building and maintaining bone strength; iron is a vital nutrient that health-conscious people who avoid eating fatty animal foods might lack; and zinc helps to build strong bones, while speeding up recovery from muscular injuries. Cardiovascular fitness is central to any exercise regime: you're not only protecting your heart, but also increasing its capacity to keep you going. Many of the nutrients in green beans work together to keep blood vessels strong, flexible, and unimpeded by cholesterol deposits. This allows blood to move oxygen and nutrients around your body fast, keeping you at peak strength and energy.

CHINESE BEANS

1lb. green beans, cut into
  finger-length pieces
1 tbsp. peanut oil
1 garlic clove, crushed
2-in. piece gingerroot, finely
  chopped
1 tbsp. peanuts, chopped
1 tbsp. soy sauce

Steam the beans until they are just tender; set aside. Heat the peanut oil and briefly stir-fry the garlic and ginger. Add the beans and peanuts and stir-fry 2 to 3 minutes to heat through. Add the soy sauce and serve immediately.

spinach

Eat this powerful vegetable for strength, energy, and stamina. It guarantees you will be fighting fit.

NUTRIENTS

Vitamins B2, B3, B6, C, E, K, beta carotene, folate; calcium, copper, magnesium, manganese, iron, phosphorus, potassium, selenium, zinc; fiber; omega-3 oils; protein; tryptophan

The strength of spinach lies in its rich content of a large number of nutrients that work together. It is an excellent source of iron, but is equally rich in vitamin C, which helps the body to use iron efficiently. Similarly with calcium, magnesium, and vitamin K, which all help build and maintain bone strength. It's a myth that the oxalate content prevents the body absorbing calcium: it just contains far more calcium than the oxalates can bind. Just 2 tablespoons cooked spinach contain more than the daily requirement of vitamin K and most of the beta carotene you need.

EASY EGGS FLORENTINE

1lb. spinach
½ tsp. vinegar
4 eggs
4 tbsp. grated cheese
black pepper to taste

Put the spinach in a pan with the lid on tightly and cook over low heat 2 minutes until it wilts. Bring a pan of water to a boil and add the vinegar. Carefully break the eggs into the water and poach them 3 minutes. Put the spinach in a baking dish and place the eggs on top. Sprinkle cheese over and melt under a hot broiler. Season and serve as it is or on toast.

black bean

It's no wonder people say you're "full of beans" when they can see you've got energy to spare.

When you're working out regularly, it's important to eat high-protein foods that build and preserve muscle. As vegetarians know, this doesn't have to be meat. Beans are a healthy alternative, providing a dose of protein with a very low fat content. Black beans are also rich in nutrients, such as iron, that increase energy levels, which, in turn, helps to feed the muscles with oxygen. They are also packed with soluble fiber to stabilize blood sugar and maintain stamina. Beans with brown rice is an ideal meat-free, protein-rich meal.

NUTRIENTS
Vitamin B1, folate; iron, magnesium, manganese, molybdenum, phosphorus; fiber; protein

EASY BLACK BEANS

2 sweet potatoes, chopped
2 tbsp. peanut oil
2 onions, roughly chopped
1 tsp. cumin
4 cloves garlic, crushed
2 bell peppers, seeded
   and diced
1 can (15-oz.) black beans,
   drained

Boil the potatoes 10 to 15 minutes; reserve the water. Heat the oil and fry the onions 2 to 3 minutes. Add the cumin and garlic and stir-fry 1 minute. Add the peppers and stir-fry for 3 minutes. Add the beans and 4 tablespoons sweet-potato water. Bring to a boil and simmer 5 minutes, adding the potato for the final minute. Serve.

lentil

NUTRIENTS
Vitamin B1, folate; copper, iron, manganese, molybdenum, phosphorus, potassium; fiber; protein

DHAL

1 tbsp. peanut oil
1 tsp. mustard seeds
1 large onion, finely chopped
2 cloves garlic, crushed
1 tsp. ground cumin
1-in piece gingerroot, finely chopped
1 cup lentils

Heat the oil and fry the mustard seeds until they pop. Add the onion, garlic, cumin, and ginger and stir-fry 3 to 5 minutes until the onion is soft. Add the lentils and 3½ cups water and bring to a boil. Simmer 30 to 40 minutes. Serve with bread or rice, or refrigerate overnight and reheat to serve.

Packed with minerals and complex carbohydrates, lentils build strength and endurance.

It's vital to choose the right kind of snack before exercising. Lentils provide the perfect combination of nutrients to allay hunger pangs and spark long-lasting energy. A spoonful of dhal on bread, for example, is sustaining but not heavy, so it won't slow you down or cause indigestion. Lentils are rich in complex carbohydrates, which the body turns into glucose, providing a steady source of energy. They also contain iron, and plenty of protein with very little fat.

Lentils help improve blood circulation, keeping muscles oxygenated during exercise.

○ ◑ ♥ Ⓖ ≡

pumpkin seed

These nutritious nibbles help your joints, heart, and circulation keep up when you're keeping fit.

Exercise requires good circulation, and pumpkin seeds are rich in a compound that can help. Pumping oxygenated blood rapidly around the body puts pressure on the arteries, which need to remain flexible and clear. Pumpkin seeds are one of the richest natural sources of phytosterols, which reduce the risk of arteries becoming narrowed by cholesterol. As well as being a rich source of many minerals, they contain omega-3 oils, which are anti-inflammatory and protect joints from damage during high-impact activities, and promote healing if you get injured while playing a sport or exercising.

NUTRIENTS

Vitamin K; copper, iron, magnesium, manganese, phosphorus, zinc; omega-3 oils; protein

VEGAN PESTO

¾ cup pumpkin seeds
4 cloves garlic
2 tbsp. olive oil
generous handful basil leaves
1 tsp. ground black pepper

Blend the seeds, garlic, and oil in a food processor until well mixed. Add more oil for a smoother texture if you like. Add the basil and blend. Add the pepper and serve with freshly cooked pasta.

045

wheat germ

This grain gives the energizing benefits of whole cereal, without causing an energy spike and slump.

NUTRIENTS
Vitamins B1, B6, E, folate; magnesium, manganese, zinc

A handful of wheat germ trail mix provides endurance and energy when you're hiking.

Wheat germ is the heart of the cereal, containing many of its most valuable nutrients. It's rich in powerful antioxidants called phenolics, which protect the cells from damage that can be caused by exercise. It also contains cysteine, which helps keep the lungs clear and functioning at their peak. Its other vitamins and minerals contribute to boosting energy and endurance. Wholewheat bread and flour contain wheat germ. But it is missing from white bread and standard baking products, which is why these provide a quick energy rush followed by a slump.

TRAIL MIX

1 tbsp. pumpkin or sunflower seeds
1 tsp. sesame seeds
2 tsp. slivered almonds
1 tbsp. wheat germ
1 tbsp. raisins
1 tbsp. finely chopped dried apricots

Mix together all the seeds and nuts and shake well. Mix in the wheat germ, raisins, and dried apricots. Eat as a snack or serve on cereal.

cashew nut

This instant and nutritious snack replenishes mineral supplies while you burn off the fat.

There is no handier snack than a packet of nuts when you've worked up an appetite exercising. Cashews are packed with minerals essential to fitness: magnesium keeps bones strong while combating muscle fatigue and soreness; copper not only increases energy and protects joints from injury, but also helps the body to utilize iron. You're still burning calories fast an hour or so after a workout, so enjoy some cashews rather than an empty-calorie snack. They're rich in monounsaturated fats, which bring a lot of heart-strengthening benefits.

NUTRIENTS
Copper, magnesium, phosphorus; monounsaturated fats; tryptophan

CHICKEN WITH CASHEWS

1 tbsp. peanut oil
2 bird's-eye chilies, seeded and chopped
2-in piece gingerroot, finely chopped
3 cups cubed marinated chicken (see p.60)
2 scallions, chopped
2 tsp. vinegar
2 tsp sesame oil
heaped 2 tbsp. cashew nuts

Heat the peanut oil and briefly stir-fry the chilies and ginger. Add the chicken and stir-fry 2 to 3 minutes. Add the onions, vinegar, and sesame oil and fry 5 minutes, checking that the chicken is well cooked. Transfer to a bowl. Stir-fry the cashews 1 minute and sprinkle over the chicken. Serve with rice.

chicken

NUTRIENTS

Vitamins B3, B6; phosphorus, selenium; protein; tryptophan

This popular meat is a power-pack of lean protein and a provider of B vitamins to give you a blast of sustained energy.

EASY CHICKEN MARINADE

3 tbsp. soy sauce
3 tbsp. rice wine or dry sherry
1 tsp. sugar
2 cloves garlic, crushed
3 cups chicken breast, cut into
   bite-size pieces

Mix together the soy sauce, wine, sugar, and garlic. Place the chicken in a dish, pour the marinade over, cover, and place in a cool place for 2 hours.

Lean meat is a top choice for anyone doing regular exercise, and organic chicken is one of the leanest, as long as you resist eating the skin. It provides a healthy dose of protein to build strength and keep bones strong, along with a pair of vitamins that maximize its energy value. Niacin and pyridoxine, or vitamins B3 and B6, work together to make the most of food's energizing potential. Chicken should always be bought organic: it is now widely available, and provides all the benefits without the risk of food-poisoning bacteria and drug residues.

◎ ⓒ ◉

cheese

Don't pass on the cheese: this nutritious food can build up your bones and muscle strength, without adding anything to your weight.

NUTRIENTS
Calcium, iodine, phosphorus, selenium; protein

Weight-bearing exercise builds strong bones, but it puts them under pressure, increasing the body's need for foods to build bone density. Famous for its high levels of calcium, cheese also contains phosphorus, which combines with calcium to strengthen the bones. It is also packed with protein, which builds muscle strength. Unfairly maligned as a high-fat food, cheese can be bought in a wide range of low-fat versions that are still nutritious. As with other products of animal origin, organic is best.

Eating cheese increases the body's ability to burn fat after a meal.

WELSH RABBIT

4 slices bread
1 tbsp. peanut oil
1¼ cups grated Cheddar cheese
1 tbsp. brown ale
½ tsp. mustard
black pepper to taste

Toast the bread under a broiler. Heat the oil in a pan and add the cheese, ale, and mustard. Stir over a low heat until thick. Season with pepper and spoon over the toast. Put back under the broiler until the cheese bubbles. Serve immediately.

egg

Little capsules of strength and energy, eggs are rich in nutrients that will maximize your workout gains.

Eating the right meal within an hour or two after exercise can make the biggest difference you've noticed yet. That's the time when your body needs—and most effectively uses—food to turn your effort into stronger muscles and increased energy levels. It's also when you burn fat most effectively. Eggs are a concentrated source of muscle-building amino acids and other body-building nutrients. They're also rich in vitamin K, which helps to heal bruises and other minor sports injuries. This vitamin works by insuring blood is able to clot normally, so it can reduce the danger of blood clots in arteries.

LEEK AND PEPPER OMELETTE

1 tbsp. peanut oil
1 leek, finely chopped
1 bell pepper, seeded
   and diced
4 eggs
salt and pepper to taste

Heat the oil and gently fry the leek 2 to 3 minutes until half cooked.

Add the bell pepper and cook 2 minutes; remove the vegetables with a slotted spoon and set aside. Beat the eggs in a bowl and add 2 tablespoons cold water. Season and pour the mixture into the pan. Add the vegetables and cook around 5 minutes until the omelette is set.

tomato juice

Mineral-packed, this is the perfect post-workout drink and a healthy alternative to excessive water.

A tomato is packed with vitamins and minerals, but it is most renowned for the life-saving properties of a versatile phytonutrient called lycopene. Unusually, lycopene is unharmed by food processing, which means that tomato-based products offer many of the same benefits as the fresh fruit. A bottle of tomato juice keeps minerals at a safe level when you're running. Most of us get too much sodium in our diet, but a long run can dangerously reduce the body's levels of minerals, particularly sodium—especially if you've drunk a lot of water. A drink of bought tomato juice replenishes fluid and sodium.

NUTRIENTS
Vitamins A, B-complex, C, E, K, folate; chromium, copper, iron, magnesium, manganese, molybdenum, phosphorus, potassium; fiber; lycopene; protein

CHILLED TOMATO SOUP

8 tomatoes, skinned, seeded
   and chopped
2 cucumbers, diced
1 qt. tomato juice
2 bell peppers, seeded
   and diced
2 cloves garlic, crushed
1 tbsp. red wine vinegar
1 tbsp. olive oil

Blend half the tomatoes, half the cucumber, the juice, bell pepper, garlic, and vinegar in a blender. Stir in the oil and remaining tomatoes and cucumber. Chill 30 minutes before serving.

◉ ✋ ♥ Ⓒ ◉ ≋

grapefruit

NUTRIENTS
Vitamin C, beta carotene, folate; potassium; fiber; liminoids

A daily glass of grapefruit juice can significantly reduce the risk of kidney stones.

Eating a grapefruit at the start of a meal can help to stop you piling on the pounds.

Starting a meal with half a grapefruit is an old diet trick that does seem to work, according to scientists. In 2006, they found that this simple change helped a group of very overweight volunteers to lose weight. Their blood-sugar levels were healthier than usual afterward, too. Other evidence suggests that eating grapefruit can steady insulin levels. So they can help to prevent the vicious cycle in which gaining weight leads to diabetes, and diabetes makes people put on even more weight. Grapefruit is full of flavonoids that repair cell damage, combat cancer, and protect the heart.

GRAPEFRUIT AND CHICKEN SALAD

2 grapefruit, unpeeled
4 tbsp. honey vinaigrette (see p.29)
2 cups shredded cooked chicken
4 bell peppers, seeded and cut into rings

Grate the grapefruit peel and add to the vinaigrette. Pour over the chicken pieces. Peel the grapefruit and cut into wheels. Put the grapefruit wheels and the pepper rings into a dish and pile the chicken on top.

pear

Sweet and satisfying, pears are rich in fiber that helps the body shed excess weight.

NUTRIENTS
Vitamin C; copper; fiber

Both soluble and insoluble fiber help to fill you up in a healthy way. Pears are among the few fruits that contain a high quantity of insoluble fiber, which gives them an enticing edge, both sweet and satisfying. Their sweet taste and refreshing juiciness make them an appealing option to anyone who has given up sugary treats to lose weight. Also, when people are trying to lose weight, the change in diet sometimes disturbs the eliminatory system. Pears counteract any tendency toward sluggish digestion if you're eating less than usual.

BROILED PEARS

4 ripe pears, halved and cored
2 tbsp. dried currants
4 tbsp. apple juice

Broil the pears under low heat about 5 minutes, turning once. Sprinkle the currants on top and pour the apple juice over. Serve immediately.

◎⑫◎🖐♥©👁〰

galia melon

NUTRIENTS
Vitamins B3, B6, C, beta carotene, folate; potassium; fiber

A mouthwatering slice of nutritional goodness that tops up your antioxidant levels, too.

The dense texture of these fragrant melons makes them a satisfying replacement for the foods you're limiting, just as their sweetness meets the need otherwise filled by empty-calorie snacks. And a galia melon—also known as a rock or musk melon—contains more nutritional power than a plateful of bakery goods. Just one slice of melon provides more vitamin C and beta carotene than your body can use in a whole day. This kind of melon loses some of its vitamin C content quite quickly after cutting, so don't cut any more than the slice you're about to eat.

MELON AND GINGER

2 small galia melons
2 tsp. lime juice
1-in piece gingerroot, finely
   chopped
2 tsp. cinnamon
4 tbsp. cherries (optional)

Quarter the melons and cut away the skin; discard the seeds. Cut into wedges or scoop into balls. Add the lime juice and ginger and mix together. Dust with cinnamon, top with cherries, if using, and serve.

⊙ ⚛ 🖐 ♥ ⓒ 〰

strawberry

This delicious and popular fruit contains a treasury of fat-fighting nutrition.

Strawberries are the sort of fruit people eat for pleasure, not to achieve their diet or health goals. So, it's surprising to learn that they're packed with nutrients that aid weight control, along with many other healthy effects. Their unusually rich supply of vitamins and minerals keeps energy levels high, reducing the urge to nibble. This delectable, bite-size, finger-friendly fruit is a great replacement for candy when you want a treat. And with more insoluble fiber than many other fruit, strawberries keep you fuller for longer.

A pinch of pepper adds a tasty edge to fresh strawberries.

NUTRIENTS
Vitamins B2, B5, B6, C, K, folate; copper, magnesium, manganese, iodine, potassium; anthocyanidins; flavonoids; fiber; omega-3 oils; ellagic acid

STRAWBERRY DELIGHT

4 mandarins
12oz. strawberries, dehulled
6oz. grapes
4oz. slivered almonds
2 tbsp. orange juice (optional)

Divide the mandarins into segments. Place in a serving bowl and add the strawberries, grapes, and almonds. Pour the orange juice over, if using, and mix well. Serve.

zucchini

This energizing food makes salads more substantial and keeps blood sugar steady.

NUTRIENTS

Vitamins B1, B2, B6, C, K, beta carotene, folate; copper, magnesium, manganese, phosphorus, potassium; fiber

The numerous vitamins and minerals in zucchini, or courgettes, help to keep energy levels up while your food intake is down. It is particularly rich in manganese, which helps to regulate blood-sugar levels. Refined foods and sweet products make blood-sugar levels rise sharply, providing a quick burst of energy followed by a slump. Zucchini are high in fiber, which delays hunger pangs. They can be cooked in numerous ways or eaten raw as a snack or in salads.

Zucchini replace much of the beta carotene wiped out by smoking and drinking alcohol.

RATATOUILLE

2 eggplants, chopped into chunks
2 tbsp. olive oil
2 onions, chopped
3 cloves garlic, crushed
4 zucchini, chopped
2 cans (15-oz. each) tomatoes

Sprinkle the eggplants with salt; leave 30 minutes, then rinse and dry. Heat the oil in a pan and fry the onions and eggplants 5 minutes. Add the remaining ingredients, bring to a boil, and simmer 10 minutes until the zucchini are tender. Serve.

pea

These popular vegetables are little balls of nutrient energy, packed with fiber to keep hunger at bay.

Green peas are packed with all kinds of nutrients. They are exceptionally rich in fiber, one of nature's biggest aids to weight control. Scores of medical studies show that the more fiber you eat, the less likely you are to put on weight and the more readily you will lose it. By slowing down the rate at which food moves on from the stomach, it helps to keep blood-sugar and insulin levels steady. And it may also affect hormones in the intestine that control the appetite. Peas are rich in both soluble and insoluble fiber, helping to fill you up while keeping your digestive system healthy.

NUTRIENTS
Vitamins B-complex, C, K, beta carotene, folate; copper, iron, magnesium, manganese, phosphorus, potassium, zinc; fiber; protein

PEAS WITH MINT AND ORANGE

1 cup frozen peas
1 tsp. grated orange peel
1 tbsp. orange juice
1 tbsp. chopped mint leaves
salt and pepper to taste

Bring a pan of water to a boil and add the peas and orange peel; cook 3 minutes until tender. Drain, add the orange juice and briefly heat. Stir in the mint leaves, season, and serve.

garlic

Keeping weight down is just one of this wonder-working bulb's health-enhancing abilities.

Garlic is known for its powerful smell and taste, but its protective powers are even stronger, ranging from fighting cancer to promoting weight loss. Its strongest properties stem from a rich supply of compounds containing sulfur, which is what creates that distinctive smell.

After crushing garlic, wait 10 minutes before cooking it to increase the nutritional benefits.

GARLIC SOUP

2 tbsp. olive oil
4 cloves garlic, crushed
2 cups fresh breadcrumbs
1 qt. hot vegetable stock
4 eggs (optional)

Heat the oil in a pan over a low heat and sauté the garlic about 30 seconds. Add the breadcrumbs and sauté 1 minute. Stir in the stock and bring the soup to a boil, then simmer 10 minutes. Break the eggs, if using, directly into the soup and poach about 3 minutes. Serve immediately with crusty bread.

Slimming aid

Allicin, a component of garlic, has been found to aid weight loss even if you make no other changes to your diet. At the same time, it lowers blood levels of insulin, reducing the risk of weight-related problems, such as metabolic syndrome and diabetes. Garlic doesn't just discourage fat from clinging to your hips and thighs: even more importantly, it helps to prevent fatty deposits forming inside your arteries, where they gradually harden and restrict blood flow. People who are trying to lose weight often eat high-protein diets and take extra exercise. Both of these can set up an inflammatory response in the body, which can reduce resistance to disease. So add a clove of garlic a day to your diet, as it has been proved to counteract inflammation.

Taste the difference

Garlic helps to make low-calorie meals more tasty, providing added flavor with virtually no calories. Meanwhile, it also protects the heart, lowers blood pressure, combats numerous cancers, and fights all kinds of infections.

GARLIC MUSHROOMS

2 tbsp. olive oil
4 cloves garlic, crushed
1lb. mushrooms
4 slices wholewheat bread
  (optional)

Heat the oil in a pan over low heat and stir in the garlic. Add the mushrooms and cover with a tightly fitting lid. Cook over very low heat about 8 minutes, shaking occasionally, until the mushrooms are tender. Toast the bread, if using, pile the mushrooms on top and serve immediately.

arugula

This decorative little leaf is one of the most nutritious ingredients you can find in a salad.

NUTRIENTS

Vitamins B-complex, C, K, beta carotene, folate; calcium, iron, magnesium, manganese, phosphorus, potassium, zinc; fiber

---

TRIPLE-TASTE SALAD

12 butterhead lettuce leaves
4oz. arugula leaves
4oz. curly endive or raddichio
1 tbsp. walnut oil
1 tbsp. vinegar

Tear the lettuce leaves and mix together with the arugula and curly endive. Mix together the oil and vinegar and pour over just before serving.

Salad is an ideal low-calorie meal, not least because the raw ingredients encourage you to eat slowly. This gives the body time to register when you've had enough, instead of 10 minutes later, which can happen if you eat quickly. The peppery taste of arugula (also known as rocket, rucola, or roquette) livens up a leaf-based salad. The vitamins and minerals it contains work together to preserve bone health—a concern if you've cut down on calcium-rich dairy foods while trying to lose weight.

One serving of arugula provides more than the daily requirement of bone-building vitamin K.

059

chili

These fiery hot peppers can burn away some unwanted weight as they raise your temperature.

Some experts say that chilies increase the body's fat-burning ability for about 20 minutes after a meal, so you are literally burning up the food you've just eaten faster than normal. Others say that the fiery taste simply makes you eat more slowly, or that the tastiness makes food more satisfying. Whatever the reason, adding some of these hot peppers to your everyday diet does seem to aid weight control. They also alleviate chronic indigestion and kill the bacteria that cause stomach ulcers, although eating too many can lead to stomach cancer.

NUTRIENTS
Vitamin C, beta carotene; iron, potassium; fiber

ROAST CHILI RELISH

7oz. fresh chilies, seeded
1 tbsp. olive oil
4 cloves garlic, crushed
1 cucumber, finely chopped

Broil the chilies 4 to 5 minutes until the skins blister. Put in a sealed plastic bag 10 minutes. Rub the skins off and finely chop the chilies. Mix with the remaining ingredients. Keep in the refrigerator for up to 2 weeks. Use sparingly.

almond

NUTRIENTS
Vitamins B2, E; copper, magnesium, manganese, phosphorus; protein

The ideal replacement for an empty-calorie snack, almonds will keep you going for longer.

Almonds might seem an odd weight-loss choice because they contain quite a lot of fat. But when scientists put two groups of people on low-calorie diets, one of which included almonds, the almond-eating group lost 50 percent more weight and fat than the others. Almonds are rich in monounsaturated fat, which helps you feel fuller for longer, and their high fiber content helps to keep blood-sugar levels steady and prevent hunger pangs. A dozen almonds contains just 90 calories along with a burst of protein and nutrients that combine to increase energy levels.

ALMOND SALSA

2 tbsp. almonds
2 tomatoes, chopped
2 red onions, finely diced
2 tbsp. finely cut chives
1 tbsp. chopped parsley
2 tsp. vinegar

Dry-fry the almonds briefly in a skillet. Mix together the tomatoes, onions, chives, parsley, and vinegar in a bowl. Add the almonds and serve.

rye

This high-fiber, low-GI cereal star aids weight loss and combats fluid retention.

Wholegrain cereals play an important role in weight loss. Full of insoluble fiber, they score low on the glycemic index (GI), meaning they release sugar into the blood slowly, whereas refined versions have little nutritional value and cause a sudden spike in energy, then a slump. Low-GI foods have long been known to benefit health, but they have now also proved to aid fat loss, even when you eat the same number of calories as on a higher-GI diet. Rye is one of the lowest GI cereals. It's also rich in compounds that bind to water from food, which prevents bloating.

NUTRIENTS
Magnesium, phosphorus, selenium; lignans; fiber; protein

COTTAGE CHEESE ON RYE

8 slices rye bread
½ cup cottage cheese
1 tsp. finely sliced lemongrass
4 tomatoes, roughly chopped
4 gherkins, sliced

Toast the bread. Mix together the cottage cheese and lemongrass. Pile onto the toast and top with the tomatoes and gherkins. Serve immediately.

◎ ✋ ◑ ♡ ⓒ ◉

tofu

The wonder-working soybean can protect your organs while smoothing your silhouette.

Best known for its beneficial effects on women's hormones, tofu, or bean curd, can also help to maintain a healthy weight for both sexes. It's made from fermented soybeans. Among soy's many healthy components is an isoflavone called genistein, which seems to promote fat loss by reducing the size and number of fat cells. Women using soybean to treat menopausal symptoms have found it also prevented weight gain, especially on the abdomen—a common effect of the changes in hormone levels after the menstrual cycle stops.

TOFU SKEWERS

4 tbsp. soy sauce
1 tbsp. sesame oil
1 tbsp. sweet apple juice
pinch cayenne pepper
1lb. firm tofu, drained and
    cubed
4 bell peppers, seeded and
    chopped into chunks

Mix together the soy sauce, sesame oil, apple juice, and cayenne pepper and use to marinate the tofu at least an hour. Thread the tofu and peppers alternately onto skewers. Broil or bake for 5 to 10 minutes until brown, basting often with the remaining marinade. Serve.

TOFU SMOOTHIE

7oz. tofu
½ cup orange juice
½ cup mango pulp
4 apples, chopped
4 tbsp. chopped walnuts

Put all the ingredients, except 1 tablespoon of the walnuts, into a blender. Blend on low speed until the ingredients are mixed, then on a high speed until the mixture is smooth. Pour into glasses, top with the remaining walnuts, and serve.

Get the balance right

Soy reduces the risk of many diseases: cancers, heart disease, osteoporosis, and diabetes, but its powerful effects on hormones could stimulate hormone-dependent cancers or thyroid problems, so it should not be overused. Traditional Asian foods such as tofu, miso, and natto are the healthiest option; the long-term effects of new products are not known.

Soy's healthy effects are stronger in tofu than in other soy products.

063

tuna

NUTRIENTS
Vitamins B1, B3, B6; magnesium, phosphorus, potassium, selenium; omega-3 oils; protein; tryptophan

This is a low-fat, high-protein food with a secret ingredient to aid weight control.

Popular sources of protein, such as meat products and hard cheese, are often high in fat. Yet, high-protein foods keep you going longer before flagging energy levels send you in search of a snack. Tuna is an excellent low-fat option. It's one of the richest sources of protein, providing more than even the healthiest meat. The best choices are albacore, skipjack, or yellowfin tuna. And fresh tuna is rich in omega-3 oils. Among its many other benefits, omega-3 stimulates production of a hormone called leptin that controls the appetite.

BAKED TUNA

4 fresh tuna steaks
black pepper to taste
3 tbsp. olive oil
2 onions, chopped
½ cup dry white wine
4 tomatoes, chopped

Heat the oven to 425°F. Put the tuna in a baking dish and rub with the pepper and 1 tablespoon of the oil. Heat the remaining oil in a skillet and sauté the onions 3 to 5 minutes. Add the wine and tomatoes and bring to a boil. Pour over the tuna and bake 15 minutes until the tuna is cooked through. Serve.

cottage cheese

Rich in protein and calcium, this has all you want from dairy food without the high fat content.

Dairy foods are sometimes shunned because they're seen as laden with saturated fat, but they can help in losing weight. Some studies have found that a high-calcium diet decreases the body's absorption of fat, possibly causing it to be burned off faster. A ½-cup serving of low-fat cottage cheese contains more than 60mg calcium for only 1–4g fat (hard cheese contains more calcium, but up to a third of its weight is fat). Cottage cheese is also rich in protein and the bone-building minerals that can be lacking in a low-dairy diet.

NUTRIENTS
Vitamins B2, B12; calcium, iodine, phosphorus, selenium; protein

COTTAGE CHEESE AND VEGETABLE SALAD

- 1⅓ cups chopped green beans
- 4 small zucchini, grated
- 1 tbsp. lemon juice
- 1½ cups cottage cheese
- 4 tbsp. sunflower seeds

Steam the green beans 5 minutes until tender. Mix together with the zucchini and lemon juice. Top with the cottage cheese, sprinkle the seeds over and serve.

Try cottage cheese with pepper as a low-fat replacement for mayonnaise.

065

◎ ⦿ ⦿ ♡ ≋

apple cider vinegar

NUTRIENTS
Vitamin C; manganese, potassium; acetic acid; pectin

Use this vinegar to make food seem more filling and keep hunger at bay for longer after eating.

Drinking a few drops of vinegar with or before a meal has been proved to help people lose weight. Apple cider vinegar, which is rich in nutrients, has the added benefit of reducing the indigestion that can accompany a change in diet. This can cause pangs that feel like hunger even when you've just eaten. Vinegar's acetic acid content makes you feel full sooner and for longer. This feeling of satiety stems from a reduction in the glycemic index (GI) of the food you eat. Foods with a high GI (including most highly processed items) pass through your system quickly. Vinegar reduces the GI and lets food stay longer in your stomach. It also reduces the risk of a midafternoon energy slump sending you in search of a snack.

CREAMY SALAD DRESSING

2 tbsp. apple cider vinegar
2 tsp. apple juice
4 tbsp. low-fat plain yogurt
1 clove garlic, crushed
1 tsp. chopped thyme

Place all the ingredients in a bowl and whisk together. Chill and serve the dressing on your favorite salad.

green tea

This health-giving drink can reduce weight while protecting you from a wide range of diseases.

NUTRIENTS
A wide range of polyphenols

> Don't drink green tea in early pregnancy, as it can increase the risk of spina bifida.

Few foods excite scientists as much as green tea, with its phenomenal range of health benefits. It also plays a dual role in helping you shape up: firstly by increasing exercise endurance and secondly by inhibiting the action of enzymes that help turn food into fat, especially around the midriff, where stored fat increases the risk of heart disease and diabetes. You can reap its benefits from 3 to 4 cups a day. Use boiling water for the full health benefits, or slightly cooler water for a less-bitter taste.

GREEN TEA REFRESHER

2 tbsp. green tea leaves
2 cups apple or peach juice
4 tsp. honey (optional)

Pour 1 cup boiled water onto the tea leaves and brew 3 to 5 minutes; strain into a pitcher and leave to cool. Stir in the juice and honey, then pour over ice into glasses and serve.

apricot

NUTRIENTS

Vitamins A, C; carotenoids; fibre; potassium; tryptophan

Life is sweet: this juicy fruit tastes good and helps you feel good, too.

Just as popular fresh or dried, apricots are rich in the amino acid tryptophan, which the body converts to the feel-good chemical serotonin. This brain chemical lifts your mood, making you feel more optimistic, improving self-esteem, and even helping to control impulsive behavior. And it helps you sleep well, too. Some of the tryptophan is also converted to niacin, or vitamin B3, if necessary. A shortage of this can cause lethargy, so eating apricots can keep energy levels high.

APRICOT AND RICOTTA TREATS

4 tbsp. ricotta cheese
2 tsp. honey
8 ripe apricots, halved and pitted
8 almond halves

Mix the ricotta with the honey and fill the apricots with the mixture. Stud the apricots with the almond halves and serve.

068

banana

A classic comfort food that cheers you up without the after-effects of a junk-food binge.

A banana is often a favorite fruit of babies and children and in adult life can trigger feelings of being safe and nurtured. Rich in healthy carbohydrates, they're ideal when you crave comfort foods, as they feel enjoyably self-indulgent and they're stuffed with nutrients that soothe and lift your mood. A great source of vitamin B6, bananas reduce fatigue and premenstrual symptoms. They also contain potassium, to relieve irritability, and tryptophan, to ease depression and promote healthy sleep.

NUTRIENTS
Vitamins B6, C; manganese; potassium; fiber; tryptophan

BROILED BANANAS

4 bananas, peeled
4 tsp. lemon juice
2 tsp. cinnamon
2 tbsp. almonds

Slice the bananas in half lengthwise and place on an oiled baking sheet. Sprinkle with the lemon juice and cinnamon and place under a hot broiler until the bananas start to brown. Scatter the almonds over and serve.

asparagus

These slender spears are forceful weapons against lethargy and low spirits.

NUTRIENTS
Vitamins A, B-complex, C, K, folate; copper, manganese, phosphorus, potassium; fiber; protein

Give yourself a natural high by eating asparagus. They taste delicious and supply numerous minerals and vitamins, including many of the B vitamins, which play a central role in supporting brain function and the nervous system. If any of these are in short supply you can be tired, depressed, anxious or constantly on edge. This can happen very easily if you're not eating a wide range of healthy foods. B vitamins work best together, rather than individually, keeping energy levels high and supporting mental and emotional health.

ASPARAGUS WITH HONEY AND GARLIC

1lb. asparagus
1 tsp. mustard
2 tbsp. honey
2 cloves garlic, crushed
½ tsp. chopped thyme leaves

Steam the asparagus 5 minutes until just tender; drain and put on a plate. Mix together the mustard, honey, garlic, and thyme and pour over the asparagus. Serve immediately.

avocado

This creamy fruit provides healthy fats, which raise serotonin levels and keep you happy.

A low-fat diet really can get you down! Scientists have found people are more relaxed after a higher-fat meal, and even feel less pain. Some fat is also necessary for the body to absorb nutrients that can improve your mood, such as vitamin E. No wonder people eat junk foods when they're feeling low. Avocados are the healthier alternative: instead of saturated fat, they provide healthy monounsaturated fat. They are rich in tryptophan, along with vitamin B6 and folate, which helps the body turn tryptophan into the feel-good chemical serotonin.

NUTRIENTS
Vitamins B6, C, K, folic acid; copper, potassium; carotenoids; fiber; monounsaturated fats; tryptophan

AVOCADO WITH PAPRIKA

4 ripe avocados, halved and pitted
2 tsp. paprika
2 tsp. lemon juice
4 slices wholewheat toast

Remove the avocado flesh from the skins and mash with a fork. Add the paprika and lemon juice and mix well. Serve spread on wholewheat toast.

sea vegetables

NUTRIENTS

Vitamins B2, B5, K, folate; calcium, iodine, iron, magnesium; lignans

These gifts from the ocean can help to soothe away stress and put an end to insomnia by promoting peaceful sleep.

Look out for different forms of sea vegetables, such as laver (nori), wakame, dulse, and others.

Sea vegetables, or seaweeds, best known for their use in Japanese cuisine, contain an unrivaled range of nutrients that promote emotional health and keep the brain alert. They contain a wide range of minerals: magnesium helps to relieve stress-related symptoms, such as heart palpitations; calcium helps to stabilize moods; and iron provides energy to the many people—especially young women—whose iron stores are low. The wide range of sea vegetables now available are rich in iodine, which supports thyroid function. A slightly underactive thyroid, which is fairly common, especially among women, often causes depression and lethargy before any other signs lead to diagnosis.

Helping hormones

Seaweed is among the foods credited with helping Japanese women keep their legendary composure through life's changes. Seaweed contains phytonutrients called lignans, which work as

LAVER PATTIES

1lb. laver, or rehydrated cooked nori, chopped
2⅓ cups oatmeal
1 tsp. ground black pepper
3 tbsp. oil
1lb. portobello mushrooms

Mix together the laver, oatmeal, and pepper in a bowl. Using your hands, shape into 12 balls and flatten slightly to make patties. Heat 2 tablespoons of the oil and fry the cakes 2 to 3 minutes. Brush the mushrooms with the remaining oil and broil. Serve together.

a gentle form of hormone-replacement therapy. Eaten regularly, they can help to reduce stress-inducing symptoms of the perimenopause, such as hot flashes. The plentiful nutrients found in sea vegetables could also relieve sleeplessness. The calming effects of magnesium, in particular, can counteract insomnia. Along with calcium, it can also prevent the leg cramps and restlessness that keep many women awake at night after menopause.

MISO SOUP

4 tbsp. chopped dulse
2 tbsp. wakame
1-in. piece gingerroot, finely
  chopped
4oz. firm tofu, cut into cubes
3 tbsp. miso

Pour 1¼ quarts water into a pan and add the seaweeds, ginger, and tofu. Bring to a boil and simmer 5 minutes. Stir in the miso, heat for 2 minutes, and serve.

sweet potato

NUTRIENTS
Vitamins B6, C, beta carotene; copper, iron, potassium; fiber

When you're feeling low and longing for a sweet treat, this will give your mood a healthy lift.

How can something that provides all the comfort of sweetness and carbohydrates be good for you? Easy, when it's a sweet potato. This cheery tuber is packed with nutrients that help to raise your spirits. It is rich in iron, so it can offset any deficiency, especially for women during their periods, and in vitamin B6. This vital vitamin alleviates premenstrual syndrome and food cravings, as well as helping to relieve depression. It also keeps blood-sugar levels steady, helping to prevent mood swings.

BAKED SWEET POTATOES

4 sweet potatoes, scrubbed
1 cup cottage cheese
2 tbsp. chopped chives
2 tsp. chopped coriander
2 tsp. paprika
salt and pepper to taste

Pierce the skin of the potatoes 4 times. Bake in an oven at 400°F for 1 hour, or until soft inside. Mix together the remaining ingredients. Cut the potatoes open and scoop out the flesh; mix with the other ingredients and put back into the skins. Season to taste and serve immediately.

cinnamon

This revitalizing spice can sharpen your cognitive abilities and counteract mood swings.

Cinnamon has a surprisingly strong effect on the brain and moods, scientists have found. Its distinctive smell works directly on the brain to increase alertness. It has been found to help students concentrate more effectively in exams, and might slow down the onset of cognitive decline in old age. Through a different process, cinnamon also helps to prevent mood swings caused by fluctuating blood-sugar levels. And as little as half a teaspoonful a day can help to control diabetes.

NUTRIENTS
Calcium, iron, manganese; fiber

CINNAMON-POACHED FRUIT

1 cup white wine
peel and juice of ½ lemon
2 tbsp. cinnamon
4 pears, cored and chopped
8 apricots, pitted and chopped
4 tbsp. chopped dried fruit
 of choice

Place the wine, lemon juice, peel, and cinnamon into a large pan. Bring to a boil. Add the fruit and return to a boil. Reduce the heat and simmer 2 minutes; leave to stand at least 10 minutes. Serve with yogurt, ricotta cheese, or ice cream.

rosemary

NUTRIENTS
Calcium, iron, manganese;
bioflavonoids; fiber

Rosemary is for remembrance: its evocative fragrance can help to keep your memories fresh.

Rosemary has traditionally been prized for its ability to improve the memory, and it's not a myth: this herb can help to counteract a tendency to forgetfulness. A compound called rosmarinic acid improves blood circulation, increasing the flow of oxygen-rich blood to the brain. This improves all kinds of brain functions, aiding concentration and alertness. People perform better in memory tests, and have been found to be more alert, when they work in a room smelling of rosemary. And at the same time they also feel more relaxed and contented.

ROSEMARY POTATOES

1lb. potatoes, cut into wedges
2 tbsp. peanut oil
1 clove garlic, crushed
(optional)
black pepper to taste
1 tbsp. chopped fresh
rosemary

Boil the potato wedges 10 minutes until tender. Heat the oil and sauté the garlic and potatoes until the potatoes are brown and crunchy. Add the pepper and rosemary for the final minute of cooking time. Serve immediately.

sage

This fragrant herb is a wise choice to keep you mentally alert, comfortably cool, and sleeping well.

NUTRIENTS
Calcium, iron; polyphenols

Sage has several ways of improving mind and mood. It has been proved in research to increase brain power, particularly short-term memory, as in word-recall tests. It contains compounds similar to drugs that are used to combat the formation of plaques in the brain, and research is now under way to find out if it can slow the progression of Alzheimer's disease. Sage can also ease the symptoms of perimenopause. By preventing hot flashes and night sweats, it promotes healthy sleep patterns.

Sprinkle a handful of roughly torn sage leaves onto a salad to make it even more nutritious.

SQUASH SOUP WITH SAGE

3¾ cups seeded and chopped winter squash
2 cups stock
1 tbsp. oil
2 onions, chopped
4 tbsp. chopped sage leaves
black pepper to taste

Boil the squash 10 minutes, until tender. Place in a blender, add the stock, and purée until smooth. Heat the oil in a large pan. Sauté the onions 3 minutes and add half the sage for the last minute. Add the squash mixture and bring to a boil. Simmer 10 minutes, stir in the pepper and the remaining sage, and serve.

076

○ ○ ♥ ○ ◎

kidney bean

NUTRIENTS

Vitamins B1, K, folate; copper, iron, magnesium, manganese, molybdenum, phosphorus, potassium; fiber; protein

This small but powerful food provides an armory of nutrients to keep you on top form.

The humble kidney bean provides an impressive array of nutrients for combating low moods and strengthening brain function. Rich in vitamin B1, it keeps the memory sharp and its rich magnesium content promotes physical and mental relaxation. The soluble fiber keeps blood-sugar levels steady, giving you plenty of vitality while preventing energy spikes and slumps, and it provides a mineral top-up for the many women whose periods leave them short of iron. On top of that, the high protein content helps to keep your strength up.

CHILI BEANS

1 tbsp. peanut oil
2 onions, chopped
1 tsp. cayenne pepper, or 1
   fresh chili, chopped
½ lb. lean ground beef
   (optional)
1 can (15-oz.) kidney beans,
   drained
1 can (15-oz.) tomatoes

Heat the oil in a pan and fry the onions 2 to 3 minutes. Add the chili and fry for another minute. Stir in the beef, if using, and cook until brown. Add the beans and tomatoes and bring to a boil. Reduce the heat and simmer 10 minutes. Serve with brown rice.

brown rice

A versatile grain that eases stress at all ages and smooths the path through perimenopause.

Many of the nutrients that could improve mood more effectively are lost when rice is processed to become white. Brown rice still contains all its nutrients and provides selenium, which counters depression, but is lacking in most people's diets. It's also rich in magnesium, which plays a major role in reducing mood swings and easing stress. Brown rice takes longer than white varieties to digest, preventing a sudden rise and fall in blood-sugar levels and making you feel comfortably full. Packed with phytonutrients, it is particularly useful in countering mood swings and other symptoms of perimenopause.

NUTRIENTS
Magnesium, manganese, selenium; fiber; tryptophan

RICE PUDDING

1½ cups brown rice
4 tbsp. raisins
1 cup milk
2 tbsp. honey
2 tsp. cinnamon

Boil the rice 15 minutes, or until tender. Heat the oven to 325°F. Mix together the rice and raisins in a baking dish. In a pan, gently heat the milk and honey. Pour over the rice and sprinkle with cinnamon. Bake 30 minutes and serve.

brazil nut

This tasty snack contains a rare source of a mineral that can protect against depression and anxiety.

NUTRIENTS
Vitamin B1; copper, magnesium, manganese, phosphorus, selenium; fiber; protein

Can a few nuts really be the answer to depression, for some people? Brazil nuts are the richest source of a mood-boosting mineral called selenium. People whose diets are deficient in this have been found to suffer depression, anxiety, and fatigue, and to feel better when they eat selenium-rich food. In much of the world even a healthy diet can be low in selenium, because foods are often grown in depleted soil. The harmless Brazil nut contains other mood-enhancing nutrients, too, such as magnesium, which soothes stress and anxiety. Just a couple of brazil nuts are enough to meet most people's selenium levels.

HAPPY SALAD

½ lb. salad potatoes, scrubbed and halved
½ lb. baby spinach leaves
4 small bell peppers, seeded and chopped
salad dressing to taste
¾ cup Brazil nuts, chopped
1 tbsp. sunflower seeds

Boil the potatoes 10 minutes, or until tender. Put in a bowl and add the spinach and peppers. Mix together the nuts and seeds. Pour the dressing, over, pile the nuts and seeds on top, and serve.

⊙ ✋ ◑ ♥ ◓ ◉ ≡

sunflower seed

Combat fatigue, ease tension, and keep the brain working well by munching on this healthy snack.

People who are busy and stressed tend to eat badly when they most need good nutrition. Seeds of all kinds are nutritious, and easy to eat on the run; the sunflower variety is among the best sources of nutrients that support mental and emotional health. They are rich in vitamin E, which might reduce the risk of Alzheimer's and prevent stressful hot flashes. Vitamin E and magnesium also combat insomnia. They are also rich in the B vitamins, which are central to our psychological well-being. B1, in particular, helps to keep the brain alert under stress.

NUTRIENTS
Vitamins B1, B5, E, folate
copper, magnesium, manganese,
phosphorus, selenium

SUNFLOWER TOPPING

1 tbsp. peanut oil
4 tbsp. sunflower seeds
1 tbsp. sesame seeds
2 tbsp. walnut halves
1 tbsp. soy sauce
1-in. piece gingerroot, finely chopped

Heat the oil in a wok until very hot. Throw in the seeds and walnuts and fry 30 seconds, stirring all the time. Add the soy sauce and transfer to a bowl immediately. Add the ginger. Serve sprinkled on rice or stir-fries.

Sunflower seeds are also among the richest sources of phytosterols, which can reduce cholesterol.

080

flax seed

NUTRIENTS

Vitamin B6, folic acid; copper, magnesium, manganese, phosphorus; fiber; lignans; omega-3 oils

BREAKFAST BOOST

4 tbsp. flax seed
2 bananas, sliced
½ small canteloupe melon, seeded and chopped
4 tsp. pumpkin seeds
2 tsp. sesame seeds
½ cup low-fat yogurt
1 cup hulled and chopped strawberries

Place the ingredients, except for the strawberries, in a bowl and mix together well. Serve topped with the strawberries.

This tiny wonder-food, also known as linseed, can lift depression, aid concentration, increase energy levels, and smooth hormonal changes.

Whatever your age or sex, flax seed can make you feel happier and help you to think more clearly. This superseed contains nutrients that are vital to brain functioning, but are lacking in most people's diets. For women aged over 35, it can also alleviate stressful perimenopausal symptoms, such as hot flashes, insomnia, and mood swings. It also keeps the body's production of hormones and other chemicals in balance. This prevents hormonal upheaval caused by premenstrual syndrome or a malfunctioning thyroid.

Flax seed is rich in compounds called lignans, which the body converts into hormonelike substances that smooth out fluctuating hormone levels. It is also one of the richest sources of omega-3 essential fatty acids, renowned for their benefits to mind and body.

One of the ways omega-3 helps to keep the brain and nervous system working smoothly is by allowing cells to function and communicate with each other properly. This can prevent many disorders we think of as psychological. It also increases mental alertness and memory.

Getting the benefits

Flax seed contains a form of omega-3 called alpha linolenic acid (ALA), but our ability to use it is reduced by saturated and hydrogenated fats, which compete for the same receptors in our bodies. So cut down on these fats and eat foods rich in vitamins B3, B6, and C, plus zinc and magnesium, which help the body to absorb ALA. Flax seed oil is rich in omega-3, but does not contain lignans and loses much of its value if used in cooking.

1 tbsp. flax seed contains nearly all the omega-3 you need in a day.

oyster

NUTRIENTS
Vitamins A, B-complex, D, E; calcium, copper, iodine, iron, potassium, selenium, zinc; omega-3 oils

A 3-oz serving cooked oysters contains only about 120 calories.

Famed for putting a sparkle back in your sex life, these molluscs are also packed with omega-3.

Oysters are renowned for being an aphrodisiac, restoring libido to people who don't enjoy sex any more. That's partly because they're so rich in zinc, along with practically all the other minerals we need for good health. When the body is short of vital nutrients, sex is low on the list of functions it needs to maintain. Packed with nutrients, oysters act as a general health tonic, as well as enhancing sexual well-being. They are a very rich, low-fat source of omega-3 fatty acids, which make us feel happier and livelier by supporting the brain's healthy functioning. They are also full of B vitamins, essential to mind and mood.

GREEN OYSTERS

24 fresh oysters
1lb. chopped fresh spinach
2 cups chopped fresh parsley
4 tbsp. white wine

Heat the oven to 425°F. Open the oysters, remove from the shells, and wash, discarding any already open. Place on half shells in a baking dish. Mix together the spinach, parsley, and white wine. Spread over the oysters and bake 6 to 7 minutes, until cooked through. Serve hot.

milk

Stay calm but alert with a drink that can combat premenstrual symptoms.

Many women become irritable, forgetful, or depressed before a period starts—the well-known symptoms of premenstrual syndrome (PMS). A glass of milk can be the simplest answer, as it contains many nutrients that lift and stabilize mood. It's rich in calcium and vitamin D, which together have been found to reduce or even prevent PMS symptoms. As with other animal foods, it's best to buy organic. Organic milk has been found to contain up to 70 percent more omega-3 oils, which help the brain to function. Have cold milk when you need to stay awake: it triggers the brain's production of dopamine and noradrenaline, which keep you alert.

NUTRIENTS
Vitamins A, B2, B12, D, K; calcium, iodine, phosphorus, potassium; protein

CEREAL SOOTHER

2 cups wholegrain breakfast cereal, such as muesli
4 tbsp. sunflower seeds
2 bananas, sliced
1 cup skim or 2% milk

Mix together the cereal and the seeds in a large serving bowl. Serve topped with the banana and the milk poured over.

083

blueberry

NUTRIENTS
Vitamins C, E; manganese; fiber

This sometimes tart little fruit is a powerful weapon in the fight against age-related damage.

When researchers compile a list of the best foods for fighting free-radical cell damage, blueberries are usually in the top 10. Their color comes from anthocyanins, believed to combat cell damage. They contain tannin, which combats inflammation, and resveratrol, a compound that fights cancer and heart disease. A diet rich in berries has been found to protect against dementia and preserve memory and learning ability in old age. Blueberries can also help prevent urinary tract infection and keep vision clear, and they might help to reverse neurodegenerative symptoms, such as loss of balance and co-ordination.

BLUEBERRY AND PEAR CRUMBLE

¾ stick butter
¾ cup all-purpose flour
½ cup rolled oats
4 tbsp brown sugar
2 large pears, cored and sliced
4 tbsp. blueberries

Heat the oven to 350°F. Rub the butter into the flour and oatmeal

in a mixing bowl until the mixture is like bread crumbs. Stir in the brown sugar. Mix together the pears and blueberries in a greased baking dish. Sprinkle the crumble mixture over the top and cook 40 to 45 minutes until golden brown on top. Serve piping hot.

fig

A tasty fruit that contains minerals to keep bones strong, and helps a sluggish digestive system.

NUTRIENTS
Beta carotene; calcium, manganese; potassium; fiber

Fig leaves, which can also be eaten, contain compounds that lower blood fats and combat diabetes.

Two of the minerals in figs help to protect our bones: calcium, whose value is well known, and potassium. Most of us eat too much sodium (mainly from salt) and not enough potassium, which balances some of sodium's effects. While excess sodium causes the body to excrete calcium, potassium helps to reduce this loss. It also counteracts sodium's harmful effects on blood pressure. Figs' other main value is in relieving constipation, which is often a problem in later life. A compote made with rehydrated dried figs will cure it effectively.

SPICED FIGS

12 dried figs, soaked overnight 2 tbsp. raisins ½ cup red wine ½ tsp. ground cloves 2 tsp. cinnamon pinch black pepper	Drain the figs, reserving 2 tablespoons of the water. Blend together with all the other ingredients in a blender. Place in a saucepan, and gently heat 5 minutes. Serve topped with ricotta cheese or yogurt.

cherry

Bones and joints feel the benefit of this juicy treat, which might even hold the key to staying young.

NUTRIENTS

Vitamins B-complex, C; calcium, potassium; ellagic acid; flavonoids; fiber

Aching joints and fragile bones are an unwelcome symptom of aging, but cherries can do a lot to protect them. Their rich anthocyanin content acts as a powerful anti-inflammatory, combating pain in joints and muscles. This has the added benefit of helping people to stay active, which promotes general good health, as well as bone strength and physical coordination. And it is the anthocyanins in cherries that give them the same heart-protective effects as red wine.

Another way in which cherries help is by supplying the mineral boron, which might help to prevent the steady loss of bone density with advancing age.

CHERRY SALAD

1 head of romaine lettuce
1lb. cherries, pitted
2 ripe pears or apples,
   cored and chopped
1 cup cubed cheese
salad dressing to taste
½ cup walnut halves

Tear the lettuce leaves and mix together with the fruit and cheese in a bowl. Pour the salad dressing over, top with the walnut halves, and serve.

CHERRY HOT-OR-COLD SOUP

1lb. cherries, pitted
1 tsp. cinnamon
grated peel and juice of
   ½ lemon
4 tbsp. red wine
4 tbsp. honey

Blend the cherries, cinnamon, and lemon with ½ cup water. Pour into a saucepan and add the wine and honey. Heat gently over low heat for about 5 minutes. Serve hot or chilled and top with yogurt, if wished.

Sweet (and sour) dreams

Sleeplessness often comes with later age, and cherries can help there, too. They contain melatonin, the nutrient that plays an important role in promoting healthy sleep patterns; it's often used to combat jetlag. Sour cherries are even richer in melatonin than their sweet relatives. On top of all that, cherries are rich in a number of flavonoids that protect the heart and reduce the risk of cancer.

The antioxidant effects of cherries are stronger than those of most other foods.

pomegranate

NUTRIENTS
Vitamin C, beta carotene, folate; potassium; ellagic acid; fiber

An ancient symbol of life and good luck that keeps its promise in later age.

Drinking a glass of pomegranate juice a day can help to protect you against three major problems of old age: heart disease, cancer, and osteoarthritis. In men who already have prostate cancer, pomegranate has been found to slow the rate at which tumors grow. It might also reduce the risk of developing various cancers. The pomegranate's abundant polyphenols work as powerful antioxidants, preventing heart damage and buildup of plaque in the arteries. It can ease the pain and disability of osteoarthritis by slowing the deterioration of cartilage in the joints and preventing inflammation.

POMEGRANATE CREAM

¾ cup plain yogurt
2 tsp. honey
4 ripe pomegranates
4 sprigs mint

Place the yogurt in a small bowl and stir in the honey until well combined. Cut each pomegranate in half horizontally and, using a wooden spoon, bash until the seeds fall out. Mix the pomegranate seeds with the yogurt and honey mixture, garnish with mint, and serve.

⊙ ⊘ ⊙ ♥ © ⊚

eggplant

The polished purple skin of this plant has very powerful and protective qualities.

NUTRIENTS
Vitamins B1, B3, B6, folate; copper, magnesium, manganese, potassium

Some people need more iron in their diet, but too much iron isn't a good thing. It increases the body's production of free radicals, byproducts of metabolic processes that damage the cells. Eggplants contain a host of phytonutrients that mop up harmful free radicals. One of them is chlorogenic acid, a powerful antioxidant that lowers levels of harmful cholesterol and has antibacterial and antiviral properties. Another is nasunin, which can also help the body excrete excess iron. This reduces the risk of conditions such as cancer, heart disease, and arthritis.

BABA GANNOUSH

2 large eggplants
6 cloves garlic, crushed
4 tbsp. tahini
4 tbsp. lemon juice
1 tbsp. olive oil
bunch parsley

Heat the oven to 375°F. Bake the eggplants on a baking sheet 30 minutes; slice in half. Scoop out and chop the insides. Leave in a colander to drain at least 10 minutes. In a bowl, mash the eggplant with the garlic, tahini and lemon juice until a smooth paste. Pour olive oil over and sprinkle with parsley. Serve with bread and crudités.

cabbage

NUTRIENTS
Vitamins A, B1, B2, B6, C, K, folate; calcium, magnesium, manganese, potassium; fiber; omega-3 oils; protein

One plant carries a whole arsenal of weapons to defend against cancers and Alzheimer's.

As a cruciferous vegetable, cabbage fights cancer on many fronts. Its various compounds help the liver remove toxins, stop cells proliferating and prevent oestrogen from stimulating the growth of breast cancers. It also combats arthritis and eye disease. Red cabbage is richest in vitamin C and cancer-protective phytonutrients and can protect against Alzheimer's. Its anthocyanins counteract the effects of a chemical called beta-amyloid protein, which can damage brain cells. Let cruciferous vegetables stand for a few minutes after chopping, as this creates many healthy compounds.

CABBAGE AND APPLE SALAD

2 cups shredded red cabbage
2 cups shredded green cabbage
2 tbsp. olive oil
1 tbsp. lemon juice
1 clove garlic, crushed
4 apples, chopped

Mix together the shredded cabbages, olive oil, lemon juice, and garlic in a large bowl; refrigerate at least 2 hours until ready to serve. Add the apple, season if desired, and serve immediately.

leek

The benefits of the life-extending allium family with a milder taste.

NUTRIENTS
Vitamins B6, C, folate; iron, manganese; fibre

Being a member of the same family as onions and garlic, the leek shares many of those vegetables' life-saving qualities. Eaten regularly, they help to bring blood pressure down to healthy levels. They also reduce the risk of stroke and heart disease by combating harmful LDL cholesterol and increasing levels of the "good" cholesterol, HDL. This helps to keep the arteries clear and supple by preventing a buildup of plaque. They also combat prostate and colon cancers, both reducing the risk and slowing the growth of tumors. Leeks contain less of the protective compounds than onions or garlic, but their milder taste allows them to be eaten in larger amounts.

Lightly steamed leeks are perfect to offset the oiliness of omega-3-rich fish.

LEEK AND POTATO SOUP

3 tbsp. olive oil
2 cloves garlic, crushed
2 potatoes, peeled and grated
3 cups sliced leeks
1 qt. stock
pepper to taste
2 tbsp. chopped parsley

Heat the oil in a skillet and fry the garlic 1 minute. Add the potatoes and leeks and sauté 5 to 10 minutes. Add the stock and bring to a boil. Reduce the heat and simmer 30 minutes; blend if desired. Stir in pepper, garnish with parsley, and serve.

◎ ✤ ♥ ⒸⓍ ◉ ≋

lettuce

NUTRIENTS
Vitamins B1, B2, C, K, beta-carotene, folate; chromium, iron, manganese, molybdenum, phosphorus, potassium; fiber

PEAS AND LETTUCE

½ stick butter
2½ cups peas
8 large romaine lettuce
leaves, cut into strips
4 tbsp. stock or water
1 tsp. pepper

Melt the butter over low heat. Add the peas and lettuce, and the stock or water and bring to a boil. Cover and simmer 5 minutes. Season with pepper and serve.

Add a lettuce leaf to that sandwich and divide your risk of a hip fracture in half.

It looks insubstantial, but a lettuce leaf could be a powerful protector against one of the most frequent accidents that disable older people. Scientists have found that older women who eat lettuce every day have half as many hip fractures as those who eat it less than once a week. It's the vitamin K content that does so much good. Any kind of lettuce helps, but, as with other leafy foods, the darker color is a sign of more nutritional value.

> The dark green leaves of the romaine are the most nutrient-rich of all lettuces.

mushroom

All kinds of mushrooms are now known to combat cancer and age-related diseases.

Mushrooms are one of the richest sources of a powerful antioxidant called L-ergothioneine, which combats cell damage. They are also rich in vitamin B3, which might slow the onset of age-related dementias, and potassium, which helps to regulate blood pressure. Research is being done into their cancer-fighting properties, including reducing the risk of breast cancer. And their minerals can ease the pain of arthritis. Mushrooms might also help to slow down age-related muscle loss, as they provide protein in a form that the body can easily use. Shiitake mushrooms, in particular, are rich in iron.

NUTRIENTS
Vitamin B-complex, biotin, folate; copper, manganese, phosphorus, potassium, selenium, zinc; protein; tryptophan

BLACK AND WHITE MUSHROOMS

½ tbsp. olive oil
8 large portobello mushrooms
4 slices wholewheat bread
2oz. halloumi cheese
1 tbsp. soy sauce

Place the mushrooms face-down on a broiler pan and brush lightly with oil. Broil 3 minutes until tender; repeat on the other side. Meanwhile, toast the bread in a toaster. Top 4 of the mushrooms with halloumi cheese and broil 2 minutes. Pour soy sauce onto the remaining mushrooms. Serve on the toast.

olive

Snack on olives to keep your skin youthful, while oiling your joints and protecting your cells.

Olives, and their extra-virgin oil, are among the best sources of monounsaturated fats. They are also rich in vitamin E and polyphenols. These three nutrients are associated with a lower risk of colon cancer, which becomes increasingly common in later age. Together, these nutrients protect cells from the damage that can lead to cancer, as well as causing heart disease, hardening of the arteries, and skin deterioration. Their soothing effects on tissue can ease the pain of arthritis. The vitamin E content can reduce the severity of hot flashes.

NUTRIENTS
Vitamin E; calcium, copper, iron; polyphenols; fiber

TAPENADE

7oz. olives, pitted and
 chopped
4 tbsp. capers, drained and
 chopped
1 can (2-oz.) anchovies,
 chopped (optional)
juice of 1 lemon
1 tsp. ground black pepper
2 tsp. olive oil

Place all the ingredients in a bowl. Mix well, or briefly blend in a blender for a smooth texture. Serve on fresh bread or as a dip with crudités.

chard

This leafy life-enhancer adds a beauty secret to its health-protective qualities.

Chard, or Swiss chard, is one of those leafy dark green superveg that counteracts many of the ills of middle and later age, including various cancers. It contains an unusually high number of vitamins and minerals. Among their many other benefits, magnesium and vitamin K keep bones strong; potassium protects the heart; beta carotene prevents DNA damage; and vitamin E keeps skin young, while reducing the risk of Alzheimer's. And they all work together to be health-protective.

NUTRIENTS
Vitamins A, B-complex, C, E, K; calcium, copper, iron, magnesium, manganese, phosphorus, potassium, zinc; fiber; protein

CHARD AU GRATIN

1lb. chard
1 tbsp. olive oil
4 cloves garlic, crushed
1 can (15-oz.) tomatoes
1 cup grated cheese
2 tsp. lemon juice

Strip the leaves from the chard and chop. Slice the stems, boil 10 minutes, and drain. Heat the oil and sauté the garlic 1 minute. Add the tomatoes and cook 5 minutes. Pour over the stems in a baking dish. Top with the cheese and broil 3 to 5 minutes. Steam the leaves, add lemon juice, and serve with the gratin.

094

squash

This bright orange superveg gives a boost to the body's cellular defenses.

NUTRIENTS
Vitamins B1, B3, B5, B6, C, beta carotene, folate; copper, manganese, potassium; fiber; omega-3 oils

The solid flesh of squashes, such as butternut and pumpkin, provides a healthy dose of age-defying nutrients. Extracts from squash have been found to help ease benign prostatic hypertrophy, which bedevils many older men as the prostate gland becomes enlarged. Regularly eating squash might help to prevent it developing. Their rich array of nutrients, including beta-cryptoxanthin, counteract the cell damage that leads to cancer and heart disease. And they have anti-inflammatory properties that might relieve the pain of many age-related conditions.

ROAST BUTTERNUT SQUASH WITH CHEESE AND WALNUTS

4 tbsp. olive oil
2 cloves garlic, crushed
2 butternut squash, halved
   and seeded
1½ cups cubed cheese
1 cup walnut halves

Heat the oven to 375°F. Place the olive oil and garlic in the hollow in the center of each squash. Roast the squash for an hour until tender. Scoop out most of the flesh, leaving enough to keep the shape. Mix together the flesh with the cheese and walnuts. Place in skins, cook for a few minutes until the cheese is soft, and serve immediately.

oregano

One of the best antioxidants in the kitchen, this leafy herb helps prevent cancer and heart disease.

Herbs and fruits are among the best providers of antioxidants—nutrients that help protect the body's cells from damage caused as a side effect of natural processes. But when researchers tested dozens of different plants, they found that oregano offers four times more protection than even that antioxidant celebrity, the blueberry. Its antioxidant qualities combat the conditions of aging, especially heart disease and cancers. Oregano is also known for its antibacterial qualities, which can offer protection against food-borne diseases, which are more dangerous to older people. Freshly picked leaves are the most effective.

NUTRIENTS
Vitamins C, K, beta carotene; calcium, iron, magnesium, manganese; omega-3 oils

One tablespoon of oregano leaves provides as much antioxidant as a whole apple.

SCRAMBLE MEDITERRANEAN

1 tbsp. olive oil
2 cloves garlic, crushed
7oz. spinach
8 eggs, beaten
7oz. feta cheese (optional)
4 tbsp. torn oregano leaves

Heat the oil over low heat and sauté the garlic 30 seconds. Add the spinach and cook 2 minutes. Beat together 3 tablespoons water and the eggs and pour over the spinach.Stir continuously so the eggs cook evenly. Crumble in the feta, if using, for the final minute of cooking time. Stir in the oregano and serve immediately.

960

oats

NUTRIENTS
Vitamin B1; magnesium, manganese, phosphorus, selenium; fiber; protein

A bowl of oatmeal for breakfast can turn out to be the healthiest meal of the day.

Can something as simple as oats provide an answer to heart disease, diabetes, and stroke? Eaten regularly, all kinds of whole grains are associated with good health in older people, but oats have special qualities. They contain a form of fiber called beta-glucan, which has an exceptional ability to reduce cholesterol —cutting the risk of strokes and heart disease from blocked arteries—and to stabilize blood sugar. Other compounds in oats protect the heart and lungs, reduce the risk of cancer, and even increase the body's ability to fight off infectious diseases.

OAT CAKES

⅔ cup fine steel-cut oats
pinch of baking soda
pinch of salt
1 tbsp. olive oil

Heat the oven to 350°F. Mix together the oats, baking soda and salt. Add the oil and 2 tablespoons hot water and mix well until a firm dough forms. Roll out on a floured surface. Cut into 8 circles, place on a greased baking sheet and bake 8 to 10 minutes until brown. Serve.

097

salmon

Oily fish counteract dryness and stiffness by lubricating the joints, eyes, and arteries.

Salmon is an excellent source of omega-3 fatty acids, which counteract many of the effects of aging. By preserving brain and cell functions, they protect against numerous diseases including cancers, age-related eye disease, stroke, forgetfulness, and dementia. They also fight heart disease by lowering cholesterol and other blood lipids, preventing arrhythmia, reducing blood pressure and making blood less likely to clot. Their powerful anti-inflammatory effects ease the pain and stiffness of arthritis.

NUTRIENTS
Vitamins B3, B6, B12; magnesium, phosphorus, selenium; protein; tryptophan

SALMON IN GRAPE SAUCE

2 tsp. mustard
2 tsp. dried thyme
2 tsp. honey
4 salmon fillets
1 tbsp. olive oil
½ lb. red grapes, halved
½ cup red wine

Heat the oven to 300°F. Mix together the mustard, thyme, and honey and rub into the fish. Heat half the oil in a pan and brown both sides of the salmon; transfer to an greased baking sheet and bake 10 minutes. Heat the remaining oil in a pan and sauté the grapes 2 minutes. Add the wine, bring to a boil, and reduce by half. Pour over the salmon and serve.

✳walnut

This powerful snack protects the heart, boosts brain power, and even helps you sleep well.

NUTRIENTS
Copper, manganese; omega-3 oils; tryptophan

Walnuts have also been found to reduce the risk of developing gallstones.

SPICY WALNUTS

1 tbsp. curry paste
1 tsp. mango juice
1 tsp. cumin
1 cup walnut halves

Heat the oven to 350°F. Mix together the curry paste, mango juice, and cumin into a smooth paste. Coat the walnuts and place on an greased baking sheet and cook 5 to 10 minutes until crisp. Serve as a snack.

Eating walnuts at the end of a rich meal can counter the effects of the fat you've eaten by reducing inflammation and keeping the arteries flexible, scientists have found. Walnuts are one of the richest sources of antioxidants. They protect the heart in numerous ways, preventing arrhythmia as well as lowering cholesterol and protecting the arteries.

One of walnut's most valuable effects is in fighting inflammation. This means more than just relieving sore skin and painful joints, especially as you grow older. Inflammation plays a role in many of the most debilitating conditions of age. It hardens the arteries, causing high blood pressure, stroke and heart disease. It speeds up thinning of the bones, leading to osteoporosis. The damage caused by chronic inflammation has been linked with the development of cancers. And it is implicated in degenerative diseases of both brain and body. Eating just half a dozen walnuts a day is enough to reduce your risk.

Friendly fats
Eating nuts may reduce the risk of developing diabetes, but if you already have it, walnuts provide the right balance of fats in

your diet. Unlike most nuts, they are rich in polyunsaturated fat. They are also among the best sources of alpha-linolenic acid, a form of omega-3 fatty acid. Omega-3 helps keep cells strong and flexible, protecting against the illnesses of aging and keeping the brain in top condition. If all that's not enough to give you good dreams, walnuts promote healthy sleep by regulating the body's melatonin production.

WALNUT AND BANANA WHIRL

2 ripe bananas, chopped
1 cup plain low-fat yogurt
8 tbsp. walnuts, chopped
2 tbsp. honey

Place the bananas in a blender. Add the yogurt, half the walnuts, and the honey, and blend, on low speed at first, until smooth. Serve immediately, topped with the remaining walnuts.

◉ ⦿ ✋ ♡ Ⓒ ◉

red wine

NUTRIENTS
Vitamins B1, B6, C, E; manganese, potassium; flavonoids; polyphenols

The health-protective powers of this drink aren't just down to the relaxing effects of alcohol.

Red wine is a central element of the Mediterranean diet, credited with promoting long life and low rates of heart disease. Its nutrients reduce cholesterol and blood pressure, keep heart muscles supple, and prevent blood clots. One of these is resveratrol, which might also protect the body's cells from cancerous changes. And a glass a day has been found to reduce the risk of Alzheimer's, by preventing plaque building up in the brain. But drinking more than ½ cup a day (women) or 1 cup (men) reduces these benefits, which are outweighed by alcohol damage.

> The wine-making process makes some of the nutrients easier for the body to use.

MULLED WINE

1 bottle (750ml) red wine 1 orange, scrubbed and halved 2 tbsp. honey 1-in. piece gingerroot, finely chopped 1 tsp. cinnamon	Put all the ingredients in a saucepan. Bring to just below the boil and simmer for 20 minutes, stirring occasionally. Ladle into cups and serve.

tea

Take a tea break: the 200 active compounds in an everyday cup are working while you relax.

Ordinary tea has been found to have an extraordinary number of health-protective qualities. Tea is, surprisingly, a very rich source of the plant compounds called flavonoids that protect the heart. Only apples, onions, and broccoli equal tea's ability to reduce the risk of heart disease by 20 percent. And, for those who are already affected, just one or two cups a day might halve the risk of a second heart attack. Tea has antibacterial qualities and might combat cancers of the digestive system. It reduces the effects of stress, increases mental alertness, and can help to protect bones from osteoporosis.

NUTRIENTS
Vitamins B1, B2, B6, C, K, beta carotene, folate; fluorine, manganese, potassium, zinc; flavonoids

BARA BRITH: WELSH TEA BREAD

2¼ cups dried fruit
1½ cups black tea
1 cup brown sugar
4¾ cups self-rising flour
1 tsp. cinnamon
1 egg, beaten

Soak the fruit overnight in the tea. The following day, preheat the oven to 325°F. Mix together the sugar, flour, and cinnamon with the fruit. Add the egg and mix well. Bake in a greased 2lb. bread pan for 1½ hours. Leave to cool, then slice, spread with butter and serve.

ailments directory

ANEMIA

The first sign that you're short of red blood cells is usually weakness or exhaustion. The likeliest cause is lack of iron or vitamin B12. Young women, in particular, are at risk, especially if they have heavy periods and eat little or no meat, as the body absorbs iron more easily from meat or fish than from any other sources. Foods rich in vitamin C help the body absorb iron. If the exhaustion continues, see your doctor.

Try more:

chickpeas, mussels, venison, prunes, green beans, spinach, yogurt, eggs, sea vegetables, sweet potatoes, oysters, milk, salmon

ARTHRITIS

Osteoarthritis is caused by wear and tear on the joints, so most people have at least a few twinges by the time they reach their 50s. It might also happen earlier at the site of an injury. The degenerative disease rheumatoid arthritis is much less common, but often starts in younger people. They're different conditions, but both may respond to the anti-inflammatory effects of foods rich in omega-3, especially oily fish (although oily fish is not recommended for anyone with the form of arthritis called gout). Calcium, iron and vitamin D have shown some good effects on arthritis. A diet rich in fruit and vegetables provides many other phytonutrients that are believed to be helpful.

Try more:

turmeric, curly endive, ginger, pineapples, green beans, cherries, pomegranates, eggplants, cabbage, mushrooms, olive oil, squash, salmon

ASTHMA AND LUNG DISEASE

Foods rich in vitamin C have long been known to fight asthma and other chest diseases. Other nutrients are now known to help in different ways: magnesium, for example, helps prevent the breath-restricting spasms of an asthma attack.

Try more:

kiwi fruit, oranges, kale, onions,
red bell peppers, mustard,
mussels, rosemary, olive oil

CANCERS

Healthy eating can prevent
up to a third of all cancers,
according to the World Health
Organization. There are a huge
number of naturally occurring
phytonutrients shown to
reduce cancer risk. Fruits and
vegetables of every kind offer
slightly different beneficial
compounds.

Try more:

oranges, raspberries, carrots,
kale, onions, red bell peppers,
turmeric, mussels, venison,
apples, beets, broccoli,
cauliflower, cumin, ginger,
watercress, grapefruits, pears,
galia melon, strawberries,

garlic, rye, brown rice,
blueberries, cherries,
pomegranates, eggplant,
cabbage, leeks, mushrooms,
olives, chard, squash, oregano,
oats, salmon, red wine

CYSTITIS

Urinary tract infections, such
as cystitis, cause intense pain
and difficulty in passing urine.
They must always be treated,
as they can spread fast and
affect the kidneys. Vitamin
C combats infection, and
some foods have been found
to discourage bacteria from
sticking to the bladder wall.
These foods are a backup to
treatment, and they reduce the
risk of recurrence.

Try more:

cranberries, alfalfa sprouts,
blueberries, cherries

DEPRESSION

The body converts nutrients
into message-carrying
chemicals that have a direct
effect on our emotions.
Nutrient deficiencies can cause
psychological problems in
vulnerable people. People who
are feeling down often neglect
themselves, so the condition
is exacerbated by poor diet.
Cheer yourself up with foods
rich in tryptophan, selenium,
B vitamins and protein.

Try more:

apricots, bananas, avocados,
sea vegetables, sweet potatoes,
brown rice, Brazil nuts, flax
seed, oysters, milk

DIABETES

Foods that release glucose
slowly into the bloodstream
help to keep diabetes under

control, and can also reduce the risk of developing this disease. Avoid processed foods and, although dried fruit and juices are healthy foods, limit these too as they are rich in sugars.

Try more:

oranges, grapefruit, garlic, almond, tofu, green tea, sweet potato, cinnamon, oats, walnuts

ENERGY AND MOOD SWINGS

Fluctuating blood-sugar levels can cause mood swings and make you hyperactive one moment, tired and stressed the next. This is usually caused by highly processed or sugary foods and can lead to other health problems, including diabetes. Aim for foods that have a gently regulating effect on blood sugar.

Try more:

oranges, raspberries, kale, chickpeas, honey, prunes, black beans, lentils, grapefruit, zucchini, peas, rye, tofu, green tea, sweet potatoes, cinnamon, brown rice, blueberries, leeks, oats, walnuts

FATIGUE

If you're getting seven to eight hours' sleep a night but feel exhausted most of the time, you might not be eating all the many nutrients you need, including protein, B vitamins, and an array of minerals. This often happens when you're busy, too, and living on fast food. Or, you might be suffering from borderline anemia or depression. You probably need to improve your diet generally. Unexplained fatigue can be a sign of something more serious, so if cutting down on stress, working sensible hours and eating well doesn't help, seek medical advice.

Try more:

wheat germ, cashews, tuna, bananas, asparagus, Brazil nuts, sunflower seeds, mushrooms

HEADACHES AND MIGRAINE

These can be triggered by a number of different stimuli, from tiredness to expansion of blood vessels in the head. They can be prevented, or relieved, by foods rich in omega-3 oils, vitamin B2, magnesium, or calcium. Some migraines are triggered by preserved meat, strong cheeses, pickles, fatty foods, coffee, or the artificial sweetener aspartame.

Try more:

chickpeas, venison, cottage cheese, sea vegetables, milk

HEART DISEASE

Healthy eating is proven to play a major role in preventing or alleviating heart disease. All kinds of fruit and vegetables are especially valuable, particularly when they are replacing high-fat foods or heavily processed items that are low in nutritional value.

Try more:

kiwi fruit, onions, mussels, apples, broccoli, grapes, green beans, pumpkin seeds, cashew nuts, grapefruit, garlic, tofu, green tea, apricots, brown rice, blueberries, cherries, pomegranates, eggplants, leeks, olive oil, chard, squash, oregano, oats, salmon, walnuts, red wine, tea

HIGH BLOOD PRESSURE

Hypertension, or high blood pressure, increases the risk of heart disease and strokes. Exercise and stress-reduction can bring it down, as can losing excess weight. Avoid high-fat dishes and salty foods.

Try more:

apples, celery, potatoes, spinach, garlic, avocado, sea vegetables, figs, pomegranate, leeks, mushrooms, salmon, red wine

INFECTIONS

Viral and bacterial infections usually attack the respiratory or digestive systems. Foods rich in vitamin C strengthen the body's defences against infections, and some foods contain specific antibacterial compounds. Drinks made with apple cider vinegar or fresh lemon juice and honey can ease the common throat and head symptoms.

Try more:

cranberries, kiwi fruit, oranges, raspberries, Brussels sprouts, kale, onions, red bell peppers, basil, cilantro, chickpeas, honey, lemons, broccoli, cumin, ginger, peppermint, yogurt, garlic, chilies, eggplant, oats, oregano, tea

IRRITABLE BOWEL SYNDROME (IBS)

This distressing and sometimes painful condition can involve constipation, diarrhea, flatulence, nausea, or all of these. Bouts can be triggered by stress or by certain foods, such as dairy products, spicy foods, or the artificial sweetener sorbitol.

Tea, coffee, and alcohol can also have an irritating effect. As IBS sometimes develops from chronic constipation, it can be relieved by the same remedies: fiber-rich foods, some exercise every day, plenty of fluids, regular meals not too late in the evening, unhurried bowel movements. If flatulence is a problem, don't eat a lot of legumes.

Try more:

raspberries, apples, artichoke, cucumber, black pepper, cumin, ginger, peppermint, pears, figs, prunes

MEMORY LOSS

Forgetfulness, inability to concentrate and "brain fog" can stem from many causes, including stress and tiredness. Some nutrients are known to help keep your brain sharp at any age, including omega-3 oils and compounds in certain herbs. These may also delay or prevent mental deterioration in later life.

Try more:

sea vegetables, cinnamon, rosemary, sage, kidney beans, flax seed, oysters, milk, blueberries, salmon, tea

MENOPAUSAL SYMPTOMS

Levels of the reproductive hormone estrogen can rise and fall sharply during the few years leading up to menopause, and then decline steeply afterward. This sometimes causes disruptive symptoms, which can be alleviated through healthy eating. Phytoestrogens help to replace some of the missing estrogen. Foods rich in vitamin E can reduce the severity of hot flashes and prevent night sweats causing insomnia. Depression, fatigue, and memory loss can also occur during this time.

Try more:

rye, tofu, sea vegetables, sage, brown rice, sunflower seeds, flax seed, olive oil, chard

OSTEOPOROSIS

Building strong bones before your 30s reduces the risk that you'll suffer from this brittle-bone condition in later life. Weight-bearing exercise is vital, and getting out in the sunshine lets your body produce vitamin D, which helps turn the calcium you eat into bone. Dairy foods and oily fish also provide vitamin D.

Vitamin K and several other minerals are also important. All of these can also delay the progression of osteoporosis if you already have it.

Try more:

kale, onions, green beans, spinach, cashew nuts, chicken, cheese, peas, arugula, soy, sea vegetables, figs, cherries, lettuce, olive oil, chard, tea

PREMENSTRUAL SYNDROME (PMS)

If you feel depressed or irritable, especially during the couple of days before a period, but fine once it starts, you probably have PMS. Sugary or fatty comfort foods can make the symptoms worse, but foods rich in vitamins B6, D, and E, magnesium and calcium can help a lot.

Try more:

cottage cheese, banana, sweet potato, flax seed, milk

STOMACH ULCERS

These painful patches of damage to the stomach wall are now known to be caused by the bacterium *Helicobacter pylori*, and can often be cured by antibiotics. Ulcers can be exacerbated by stress or erratic eating habits. Some powerful antibacterial foods can reduce the risk of developing them.

Try more:

oranges, broccoli, yogurt, garlic, chilies, bananas

STRESS

The right foods can calm anxiety and irritation just as they can lift depression. Legumes, for example, contain plenty of potassium for calmness and magnesium to promote relaxation.

Try more:

bananas, asparagus, avocado, sea vegetables, kidney beans, brown rice, Brazil nuts, sunflower seeds, flax seed, tea

THRUSH

This itchy yeast infection most commonly affects the genitals. The discomfort can be eased by daubing with yogurt or bathing with diluted apple cider vinegar. Wearing loose cotton clothes and avoiding hot baths can also help. Some foods discourage the growth of yeasts, which cause fungal infections.

Try more:

raspberries, yogurt, alfalfa sprouts, cinnamon

glossary

Anthocyanin A flavonoid that gives plants a blue to purple color and has strong health-protective effects.

Antioxidant A substance, naturally occurring in many plants, believed to protect cells from damage from free radicals.

Bacteria Microscopic single-celled organisms, some of which aid bodily functions, while others can cause disease.

Beta carotene A nutrient found in fruit and vegetables, which the body turns into vitamin A.

Blood sugar, or blood glucose The form in which fuel from food is carried in the blood to provide energy to cells. A diet of highly processed foods can make blood-sugar levels fluctuate unhealthily, causing mood swings and energy slumps. The body produces a hormone called insulin to prevent blood-sugar levels rising excessively. In diabetes, the body is no longer able to produce enough insulin to regulate blood-sugar levels effectively.

Carbohydrates Starchy or sweet foods that provide energy. The body breaks them down into glucose, for immediate fuel, and glycogen, which is stored in the liver and muscles for future use.

Carcinogen Anything that can cause cancer.

Carotenoids Antioxidants, found mainly in vegetables, that have been shown to reduce the risk of many diseases (including cancers) and enhance the immune system.

Cholesterol A fatty substance made (from dietary fat) in the body and needed for purposes such as building cell walls. If too much is produced, it can line artery walls, restricting the flow of blood to the heart and brain. Low-density lipoprotein (LDL), or "bad cholesterol", increases the risk of this, whereas high-density lipoprotein (HDL) or "good cholesterol" helps remove fats from the bloodstream.

Cruciferous vegetables An exceptionally beneficial plant family including cauliflower, Brussels sprouts, and numerous dark-green leafy vegetables.

Detoxification The body's natural process of eliminating toxic substances, which can be promoted by eating certain foods.

Diuretic Something that encourages increased urination.

Enzyme A protein that facilitates the body's chemical reactions, such as digestion.

Fat One of three necessary food groups (along with carbohydrates and protein), fat is used for numerous purposes including cell maintenance and absorption of certain vitamins. Monounsaturated and polyunsaturated fats are considered healthiest. An excess of saturated fat, mainly from animal products, can cause high blood-cholesterol levels. Hydrogenated fat, found mainly in processed foods, is now considered harmful to health.

Fiber Plant matter that the body does not absorb but that aids the process of digestion. Soluble fiber is thought to help control blood sugar and cholesterol. Insoluble fiber aids elimination.

Flavonoids Plant compounds that seem to strengthen the body's ability to resist cell damage, inflammation and infection.

Free radical An unstable molecule (formed as a by-product of the body's natural functions) that may damage cells, leading to diseases, such as cancer.

Glycemic index (GI) A measure of how quickly the body turns foods into glucose. Low-GI foods are healthier, because they release glucose slowly, helping to control blood-sugar levels and appetite.

Glycogen The form in which energy is stored in the muscles for later use.

HDL See cholesterol.

Hydrochloric acid The main component of the acids that digest food in the stomach.

Hypertension High blood pressure, sometimes caused by a buildup of plaque in the arteries.

LDL See cholesterol.

Legumes Dried beans, the large seeds of several members of the Fabaceae family. Examples in this book are black beans, kidney beans, chickpeas, soy beans (in the form of tofu), and lentils.

Leptin A hormone that controls the appetite; it may be stimulated by omega-3 oils.

Lignans Antioxidant chemicals found in certain plants that, being similar in structure to the hormone estrogen, can relieve menopausal symptoms.

Lycopene A powerful carotenoid found in red fruit and vegetables.

Nitrates Food preservatives that have been linked with cancer.

Omega-3 oils (or fats, or fatty acids). A group of polyunsaturated fats, mainly found in oily fish, believed to provide many health benefits to mind and body.

Oxalates Substances occurring naturally in certain foods that, in susceptible people, can damage the gallbladder or kidneys.

Perimenopause The time leading up to and just after a woman's final menstrual period.

Phytonutrients Beneficial compounds found in plants.

Phytosterol Substances found in plants that might lower cholesterol levels.

Plaque One form, made from cholesterol and other fats, builds up on the lining of arteries and can restrict blood flow. Another form is made from protein fragments that clump together in the brain and is linked with Alzheimer's disease.

Polyphenol A form of antioxidant chemical.

Protein An essential food group, needed for the growth and repair of tissue. Abundant in foods of animal origin, but nuts, seeds, and legumes are also good sources.

Resveratrol A cancer-fighting compound found in several plants, including red or blue berries and grapes (and, therefore, red wine).

Serotonin A chemical produced by nerve cells that lifts the mood; also found in some foods.

Tryptophan An amino acid that the brain converts into the "feel-good" chemical serotonin.

index